In reading this book by Sandra Aldrich, I was impressed that a story filled with so much personal distress is, at the same time, filled with so much faith—and hope.

As a grief therapist/psychologist, I recognize the psychological value of spiritual hope. We live in a world of unaccountable politicians, unauthentic ministers, unreliable parents and undisciplined children. Add to the list broken promises, broken relationships and broken dreams and we can find ourselves not only short on hope but isolated.

As Sandra states, "I am amazed at the people who just need someone to hear their pain." And that's what this inspiring book is all about—reaching out to others with understanding. I have been touched by her pain, encouraged by her honest expression of how it feels to be alone in grief and made wiser through her practical suggestions of working through such a significant loss.

Although this book is a tragic story of the death of a loving husband and father, I found it uplifting. At the center of this story is not Don Aldrich, but a man named Jesus who died as God, providing the human race with hope and life in another world. Because of Him, we can all live forever.

Dr. John D. Canine, Director
Maximum Living
Birmingham, Michigan

Living Through the Loss of Someone You Love

One Woman's Story of Loss, Grief, and New-found Hope.

SANDRA PICKLESIMER ALDRICH

Regal Books
A Division of GL Publications
Ventura, California, U.S.A.

Published by Regal Books
A Division of Gospel Light
Ventura, California, U.S.A.
Printed in U.S.A.

Regal Books is a ministry of Gospel Light, an evangelical Christian publisher dedicated to serving the local church. We believe God's vision for Gospel Light is to provide church leaders with biblical, user-friendly materials that will help them evangelize, disciple and minister to children, youth and families.

It is our prayer that this Regal Book will help you discover biblical truth for your own life and help you meet the needs of others. May God richly bless you.

For a free catalog of resources from Regal Books/Gospel Light please contact your Christian supplier or call 1-800-4-GOSPEL.

The Scripture quotations in this publication are from the *King James Version.*
Also quoted:
NIV—Scripture quotations marked *(NIV)* are from the *Holy Bible, New International Version.* Copyright © 1973, 1978, 1984 International Bible Society. Used by permission of Zondervan Bible Publishers.

Library of Congress Cataloging-in-Publication Data

Aldrich, Sandra Picklesimer.
    Living through the loss of someone you love : One woman's story of loss, grief, and new-found hope / Sandra Picklesimer Aldrich.
        p.   cm.
    ISBN 0-8307-1396-4
    1. Bereavement—Religious aspects—Christianity. 2. Consolation.
3. Aldrich, Sandra Picklesimer. 4. Aldrich, Donald J., 1943-1982.
I. Title.
BV4908.A59   1990
248.8'6—dc20   89-48626
                                                                    CIP

Any omission of credits unintentional. The publisher requests documentation for future printings.

4 5 6 7 8 9 10 11 12 13 14 15 16 17 / 02 01 00 99 98 97 96 95 94

Rights for publishing this book in other languages are contracted by Gospel Literature International (GLINT). GLINT also provides technical help for the adaptation, translation and publishing of Bible study resources and books in scores of languages worldwide. For further information, contact GLINT, P.O. Box 4060, Ontario, CA 91761-1003, U.S.A., or the publisher.

Dedication

Countless people provided love and encouragement when we needed it. To them this book is dedicated—especially to our Michigan folks, William and Mae Aldrich of Flint and Mitchell and Wilma Picklesimer of Chelsea.

Donald J. Aldrich
April 7, 1943—December 29, 1982
The one who brought laughter to my somber world.

Contents

BOOK TWO: LEGACY OF MY CLOWN

Foreword

Books about death and bereavement have a certain fascination for those of us who have survived the ordeal. This book is no exception. Neither sympathy nor empathy fully explain the grip such literature holds on the reader. We have been there. To see one's beloved gradually deteriorate is, in a sense, to see one's own life come apart in an atmosphere of tragedy and even horror.

Yet God has a wonderful way of bringing His children through such episodes, if only they can find it. Sandra Aldrich has discovered that way, and in this vivid personal account she gives us a map that clearly marks it for all to follow. The love she and her husband shared makes a beautiful story, even after the passage of some years. More significantly, she has since turned her life around and by closing the doors on useless grief that lead nowhere, she has found peace in a new kind of service to her Lord and her fellow human beings. The deep pain of intimate loss is still there, but time has a way of soothing the bereaved by clouding the memory—except at special times. When that happens, the sufferer can only turn to God and His grace.

Each one who goes through the dark valley comes out at a different point. My encounter with death in the homegoing of my spouse occurred later in life, and was followed by an amazing and unexpected kind of resolution. Sandra Aldrich's counsel to those still in the valley is couched in rich wisdom, and gives glory to God. I pray that what she has found, the reader will also find.

—Sherwood Eliot Wirt

BOOK ONE

Living with My Clown

CHAPTER ONE

Tangled Threads

August 9, 1981
Muskegon, Michigan

The emergency room doctor used terms such as "multiple lesions" and "metastasis" as he pointed to the numerous white spots on the CAT scan plates. Translated, the words meant Don's cancer was back. And this time it was in his brain.

I saw only sadness in the doctor's eyes. "Are you all right?" he quietly asked.

I continued to stare at the pictures of my husband's brain. All right? Inwardly I was screaming.

I forced myself to appear calm. "Yes, I'm all right for *now*. That's why you must tell me *now* exactly what we're dealing with."

He looked at me for a long moment, then said, "Mrs. Aldrich, it's a Clark Four. That means it's advanced to the worst level."

Worst level? I was having trouble sorting his words.

Less than four years ago, when Don had the simple malignant melanoma removed from his shoulder, his doctor said he had nothing more to worry about. Now this doctor was saying we had everything to worry about.

I leaned forward, determined not to pinch my leg to wake myself from this terrible dream.

"So what can we *do?*"

"For now, we'll try to get the brain swelling down and make him comfortable. You said you're from the Detroit area? We can make arrangements to get Mr. Aldrich into the University of Michigan Hospital. It's imperative treatments begin soon."

Imperative? Why was my brain working so slowly?

"How much time do you think we have?" I had to ask the dreaded question.

"Metastatic brain lesions—especially of this multitude—grow very rapidly. It could be a matter of months, or perhaps only weeks. And you must know this cancer doesn't normally respond to treatment."

Doesn't normally respond? I thought of Don lying in a nearby darkened cubicle, waiting for the results of the CAT scan. I tried to keep panic out of my voice.

"Are you saying our one hope is a miracle?"

He breathed out through his mouth and then nodded. "I'm sorry. I'm so very sorry."

* * *

The doctor and I silently walked toward the striped curtain where Don waited. My thoughts bumped against one another. Don couldn't die. He was too young. And he liked to laugh too much. Only philosophical old men are supposed to be handed news like this. Clowns are supposed to live forever.

What are Jay and Holly going to do without their daddy? He's their favorite parent . . . . And they're only eight and seven. They need him. I need him! Oh, God, please don't do this.

A widow. What a strange word. This meant I was going to be part of that sad, silent group at church. I don't want to be a widow! I want to be Don's *wife*.

We were almost to the cubicle. I turned to the doctor. "After you tell him, please let us have a few minutes alone."

I'd thought if I said no! we would be spared whatever awful thing was ahead. But God hadn't been asking my permission; He'd been trying to prepare me.

The doctor nodded and then pulled back the curtain.

Don was lying very still, his right arm over his eyes, his left one still hooked to the IV that dripped the morphine-based medicine into his vein.

I hurried over to my big, blond Scotsman and gently cupped my hand around his close-trimmed beard.

"Donnie?"

His answering "Hmmm?" sounded as though it was coming from the bottom of a well. He struggled to open his eyes. Normally their deep blue color sparkled with some new joke. Now they were filled only with pain.

I took his hand, and together we listened to the doctor's comparison of the cancer to shards of broken glass scattered throughout his brain. They were inoperable.

When he left us alone, I was still too stunned to cry.

With my face close to Don's, I prayed for our heavenly Father's help. But hadn't I felt for weeks that something bad was going to happen? We were spending our fourth summer at the Maranatha Bible and Missionary Conference in Muskegon, on the shore of Lake Michigan, but even in those peaceful surroundings I couldn't lose the nagging worry. Outwardly I'd blamed the feeling on the pressure I was under while writing my first book, but I knew it was more than that.

And there in that darkened cubicle, I realized God had been trying to prepare me for the day we were now experiencing. I'd thought if I said no! we would be spared whatever awful thing was ahead. But God hadn't been asking my permission; He'd been trying to prepare me.

Within a few minutes the doctor was back, accompanied by a neurologist. Additional Xrays and scans were ordered, but only serious looks passed between the two doctors.

* * *

The next few hours were hectic. Nurses were in and out of Don's room, and more doctors came in to check his reflexes or shine the examining light into his eyes. Gradually, reality was closing around us, but we hadn't been alone long enough to talk about it. Yet by midafternoon Don's pain had eased enough that he insisted I go back to Maranatha, collect Jay and Holly from our neighbor's care and rest before coming back to the hospital that evening.

I stood by his bed for an awkward moment. Finally I leaned over, careful not to bump the IV needle, and kissed him.

"I love you, Donnie."

He read beyond the words. "I know." Then he made

an effort to be the old Don, the clown. "Now aren't you glad you didn't quit teaching last year? Looks like you're gonna need that job."

I stammered. "I don't want you worrying about *me*."

His face contorted. "Well, I do!"

Immediately my arms were around him and my face was against his neck as we sobbed together. Guilt mixed with my fears. How silly our arguments had been that summer. And oh, the selfish things we had said. Now all I could say was, "I'm sorry. Forgive me."

He nodded. "Me too. Oh, San . . . . "

* * *

As I pulled out of the hospital parking lot, I thought about our crying together. We had communicated important things with few words. No matter what was ahead, we had been able to say what we needed to. I could be thankful for that.

I dreaded telling everyone the news. How could I tell Don's dad the cancer was back? Don's mom had died from cancer a few years before. Hadn't we had enough for one family?

And how could I tell my parents? Don had always teased me saying if we ever divorced, he was going home to live with *my* mother. And they loved him just as much as he loved them. For in spite of his being Northern, his quick grin had won over even my very Southern parents.

My thoughts kept turning to Jay and Holly. I dreaded telling them most of all. They always argued over whose turn it was to sit next to Don in the restaurants. How could I tell them the doctors were saying their daddy's going to die?

Beautiful Lake Harbor Drive stretched before me, its

stately trees shading the asphalt. The four of us should be at the beach, not separated like this. Don should be playing his usual role of "Father Confessor" to the college kids there, not lying in a hospital bed. I spoke aloud, reminding God of the many people who needed Don and how young Jay and Holly were. He couldn't die!

Suddenly, the image of my arguing with the sovereign almighty God was so clear and my attitude so ugly that I started to sob. We were totally dependent upon the very One I was ordering around.

When I could talk again, I said through my tears, "I'm broken. Here are the pieces. Do what you want. Just don't leave us alone!"

* * *

At Maranatha, I drove first to Gloria and Paul Riepma's to get Jay and Holly. Their living room was filled with friends awaiting word, so I gave a brief report, but was too tired to speculate the outcome. Besides, I hadn't told my little ones. As soon as we three returned home, I sat on a low stool facing them, my hands covering theirs. Don and I had agreed this was going to be their battle too, so it was important to be honest with them right from the start.

They waited, all summer-tanned and blond, watching my face. Finally, as simply as I could, I told them about the new cancer.

Jay, the eight-year-old miniature of his father, stared at me. "Is he going to die?"

Suddenly hot tears were running down my cheeks again. "The doctor says he's going to."

Little Holly's eyes were wide. "Does God love Daddy?"

I stood up to get a tissue. "Of course He loves him. Very much."

Then she dropped the theological bomb. "If God loves Daddy, won't He make him well?"

For a long time we talked, as I tried to explain that while God *could* heal their daddy, He might allow something else to happen. I also stressed that the Lord was with us, and that none of us was being punished for being bad. I'm not sure I covered all the important points though; I'd never had to explain "for God's glory" to a seven- and an eight-year-old before.

Finally we prayed. Jay began, his voice quivering. "Please God, don't let my daddy die!"

Suddenly all I could do was hug them and cry. How small we felt. And how frightening to face a future without our beloved clown.

I slept fitfully that night. The reality had settled around me, especially after calling our families. Don's dad and Dale, one of his brothers, made arrangements to come to Muskegon immediately. I insisted *my* parents wait until I knew when Don would be transferred to the University Hospital.

As I fixed breakfast for Jay and Holly, I told them about the scheduled bone and liver scans, but inwardly I was trying to comprehend life without the one who had filled my life for over 15 years. What would it be like to have only the three of us around the table like this?

And what if I never heard Don's booming laugh again? I first heard it after an InterVarsity meeting at college. Smiling, I had turned toward the sound, determined to find the possessor of such joy. As our relationship grew, I found he met life's challenges with that same sense of humor, sometimes to my irritation. Now we were being asked to face our greatest crisis yet, one that couldn't be dismissed with a joke.

* * *

Jay and Holly were staying with "Aunt" Gloria again, so I hurried to the hospital. Don was propped up in the bed, the IV board still taped to his hand. I kissed him in greeting, and then asked if the doctor had been in, if his headaches were better, if he'd had a comfortable night. He had just as many questions for me—who was keeping the kiddos, had I called our friends at home?

Included in my report was my call to Marta Gabre-Tsadick. My writing her book, *Sheltered by the King*, with its account of her family's escape from Ethiopia had affected my life profoundly. Now all that was set aside. But Don shook his head.

"No. I want to see it finished. In fact, I want to see two things finished: the book and the Pharaoh."

The Pharaoh was a needlepoint wall hanging he had purchased because of the Egyptian material I included in my high school mythology classes. It had become a family joke though as I ripped out almost as many crooked stitches as I put in. Don already had a spot in our living room picked out for the prize hanging, so I had kept poking the threads through the canvas. The Pharaoh wasn't important either.

Don studied me for several moments, his expression a mixture of amusement and Scottish fight.

"San, remember I'm not dead yet. You've been working on both of them forever. I want to see them finished."

I could do nothing but agree.

* * *

Later that morning, Morrie Driesenga visited us. When

we had first purchased our place at Maranatha, I noticed how reserved many of the Dutch families were. That was fine with me, but Don had charged ahead, making fast friendships. Morrie was one of his golfing buddies from our lane, and the one he teasingly called "Dad."

Now Morrie greeted me, his hand outstretched in greeting. Maybe it was the fatherly, unshed tears in his eyes. Maybe I was just tired of my emotional wall. But the tears started down my cheeks again, and I said, "Oh, Morrie, I need a *hug.*"

Immediately his arms were around me, and his tears spilled onto his face. "You got it, kid. You got it."

Gradually the three of us could talk again. Don spoke first. "I can't imagine not being here at Maranatha next summer. If only the Lord would give me one more summer here—just one more summer at Maranatha . . . ."

His voice trailed off. While Morrie offered encouragement, I remained numb. The doctors said a metastatic melanoma is a rapid cancer. They were expecting him to die within a couple of months. One doctor said he could die within two weeks or last as long as six months. Was six months supposed to be a long time? They offered chemotherapy only as an effort to help us buy a little more time. Time enough to get used to the idea of death. One more summer at Maranatha. Was that too much to ask?

When Morrie left, I walked him to the elevator, thanking him for visiting. He waved that comment aside.

"Don's biggest concern is for you and the children," he said. "I hope you'll let me help in any way I can. Don said maybe you'll need some help settling all of the paper work later. I've done that for others in our church. I'd like to do that for you—if you'll let me."

The elevator doors opened and, with a quick hug, he left.

Back in Don's room, I mentioned Morrie's offer, adding a noncommittal "Isn't that just like him?"

Don nodded, but his intense blue eyes studied me. When he spoke, his voice was a plea.

"San, when this is over, *let* Morrie help you. Let them *all* help you."

* * *

Don's dad and brother Dale arrived that evening. IV tubes and brain swelling were beyond those things his dad had been able to rock away when Don was a child.

And it was difficult for Dale too. His eyes followed the clear liquid from the IV bottle, through the tube and down into Don's arm. His questions were matter-of-fact as he asked about the doctors' plans. It was good to talk, to fill the room with step-by-step plans, rather than to face that awful silence.

Dale and I had had our share of typical disagreements during the 15 years I'd been part of their family, but that was always over our different philosophies. Now we had one mutual concern: Don. Suddenly Dale became *my* brother too. No matter what was ahead, healing had begun within the family.

* * *

The next morning, at the hospital, I kissed Don in greeting and met his new roommate. After checking the IV to make sure it wasn't backing up, I pulled a chair close to Don's bed. Just then an elderly man in a navy blue suit and carrying a Bible appeared in the doorway. He introduced himself as a volunteer from something-or-other temple and wondered if he might come in and pray with us. A temple? Oh, dear. That meant he was probably charismatic. I certainly didn't want any emotional scenes.

Even as those thoughts formed, the roommate told the visitor he had his own religion. The old man accepted the comment with such gentleness that I immediately felt guilty about my own inward rejection. Don raised himself on one elbow.

"I think that's nice," was all he had to say. The elderly man walked toward us, his hand outstretched in greeting.

"What's your affliction, Brother?"

Then Don was telling the story again, complete with the doctor's insistence that our one hope was a miracle.

The man put his hand on Don's head. "Brother, I was healed from an affliction 30 years ago. I'm going to ask the Lord to heal you in that same way."

Oh, dear. As much as I wanted him to pray for healing, I was very much aware of the listening roommate. But Don's eyes were already closed. I bowed my head too.

The man began, thanking God for His power and His promises. Something about his voice transcended this pathetic world, and I no longer worried about what the roommate thought. I nodded as the man asked that Don's cancer be removed. But suddenly I was aware of another cancer: mine.

"Lord," I inwardly prayed, "my emotional cancer can't be seen, but it's just as deadly. Remove it from my attitude, Lord. Heal *me* too."

At the man's "Amen," I opened my eyes, expecting a rainbow filling the room. But it was only the same old hospital room, and the IV needle was still in Don's arm. *Something* had happened though. I felt an almost tangible Presence. God was with us—no matter what was ahead.

* * *

All week Jay had been insisting God wasn't going to let his daddy die. I certainly didn't want to discredit so great a faith, but I also knew too many cases where faith and denial had gotten confused, robbing the participants of saying important things. I didn't want our children to chant, "Daddy's going to die," but I knew the danger of expecting God to perform His miracles *our* way.

Then I remembered Corrie ten Boom's illustration with her needlepoint at the end of the movie *The Hiding Place*. She had first shown us the tangled underside, explaining that's all we see here on earth. But as she turned it over to show a golden woolen crown, she said the threads together produced the result that is seen from heaven's side—the crown of His glory.

On Wednesday morning, I spread the Pharaoh needlepoint upside down on my lap and called Jay to me. All summer he had watched as I put in the stitches and yanked several others out. He was delighted to watch the pattern take shape into something he could recognize. I sent up a quick prayer before I spoke.

"Jay, look at all of these tangled threads. It looks like one big mess, huh?"

He nodded, so I continued. "Well, life is often like that. All we see from this side on earth is the mess. Often the dark colors overwhelm the light colors, just like here. But when we get to heaven, look what happens."

I turned the needlepoint over. "See? When we get to heaven we'll see exactly what the Lord was doing. And we'll know it wasn't a mess after all. And that's how it is with your daddy's illness."

Jay stared at the intricate pattern. When he turned back to me, his eyes were bright.

"And you know what, Mom? I'll bet the *colors* God uses are beautiful ones we never see on earth either."

He leaned against me as I put my arm around him. He was going to be all right.

Holly's acceptance of the problem wasn't so easily solved. She had retreated into babyish behavior. She even started sucking her thumb at night, something she had given up years earlier. When she could visit her dad at the hospital, she was fine. But at home, she whined. I had little energy, so all I could do was give her extra hugs and let her sit on my lap whenever she needed. If I was having a rough time understanding all of this, how could I expect a child to?

* * *

The third day of Don's hospitalization, the doctors ordered the awful IV removed from his arm. To make the day even better, Marta Gabre-Tsadick and her husband, Deme, drove up from Fort Wayne. We had a wonderful afternoon together, drawing upon their spiritual strength and being encouraged by their prayers.

When they left, I handed Don his robe and insisted we enjoy the beautiful day together. He was glad to escape the room too, and leaned on my shoulder as we stepped into the sunshine. His legs were still wobbly from the days spent in bed, so we walked slowly to the picnic table behind the hospital.

We sat quietly for a few moments, enjoying the summer breezes under those big maples. Finally Don spoke. "I know you've been worrying about me. But I don't want you to forget about your book either. Seeing Marta and Deme just reinforces the importance of getting their story told."

His eyes pleaded with me not to argue, but then the

clown surfaced again. "And in your 'spare' time I don't know why you don't finish the Pharaoh. You could work on it here while you keep me from chasing the nurses."

I would have liked for him to put his arm around me in his old protecting way, but he was staring up into the deep green branches over our heads. Our roles were reversing; it would be up to me now to protect him. I took his hand, careful not to press the tender area where the IV needle had been.

* * *

On Thursday morning, when Don was scheduled for the liver scan, Jay and Holly accompanied me to the hospital. When the technician came to take Don downstairs, she invited the three of us to accompany him. I was delighted by her thoughtfulness. I'd had scans in the past because of persistent ear ringing, so I knew how boring it was just to lie still and wait for the little dots to form on the screen the image of the internal organ.

Downstairs, Don grimaced as the technician probed for a vein for the scan dye. Immediately Holly was next to him, cooing a "Oh, poor Daddy." Just two weeks before, Don had hovered over her in the adjacent emergency room as the doctor closed a gash in her leg. The staff had insisted only one parent could stay and, of course, Holly had chosen her daddy. Now she took his free hand into both of hers and whispered, "Just squeeze whenever you need to. I'm right here."

Don pulled her closer, his eyes filling with tears.

"Are you okay?" the technican asked.

He nodded. "Yeah. It's just that I always say that to her when she's hurt."

I couldn't speak for several minutes and was glad for

Jay's interest in the machine. He wanted to know what the difference was between Xrays and scans, and why the dye showed only the liver outlined and not the rest of the internal organs.

Don gave him one of his That's-my-boy looks as the technician enthusiastically explained that Xrays are sent *into* the body in order to give us a picture of what is there, while the dye used for the scans and designed for a specific organ send pictures *out.*

Then she asked, "Is he going to be a doctor when he grows up? I don't get questions like that even from adults."

Don looked at me as he answered. "I'd like that very much. I want both of them to have every opportunity to be whatever God wants them to be—no matter what happens."

I stared back at him and then nodded my promise.

* * *

In the afternoon we learned officially the liver scan was clear. But we'd seen the dots outline a normally shaped organ. Now we were ready to leave for the other side of the state—and the University Hospital—on Saturday morning.

After we received the scan report, the four of us walked outside. Don leaned on my shoulder while Jay and Holly released tension by chasing each other. When we sat down, I opened the canvas bag and pulled out the Pharaoh.

"I wonder if I'll ever be able to teach again or even play tennis," Don said. "I know that's a dream, but I can't get used to the idea of dying just yet."

I wish I could have thought of something wonderfully uplifting to say, but my leaden thoughts refused to form words. I was relieved when Jay and Holly darted by, trying to catch a cabbage butterfly. Don looked at his watch. "We ought to go back in. Ron said he'd be up this afternoon. I, uh, want to ask him how it'll be."

I jerked my head to look at him. Ron Hagelman, his tennis partner, was a doctor of nuclear medicine. Don was planning to ask him what it was going to be like to die!

I never learned the details of that conversation. Even my direct questions were dismissed with "I guess each person is different." The clown in him had never liked discussing depressing things, so of course he was taking that same attitude about something as incomprehensible as death. In his own time, he would let me know when he needed to talk.

Jay and Holly were singing that night in the musical program in the Maranatha Taberacle, so we left the hospital early. Just as I arrived back at Maranatha, two women asked about our plans to return to the other side of the state. Suddenly the tears were threatening to stream down my face, so I stammered, "I'm sorry, but I'm just so tired." How nice it would have been to have one of them put her arms around me and say it was okay to hurt. Instead she merely nodded. "Well, you're only human." *Human* was actually what I didn't want to be. I turned to go into the lodge.

Inside, friends insisted I join them in the dining hall for a cup of tea. As I sat with them, several others stopped to remind me of their prayers. I watched the rain streak down the window, thinking how appropriate the weather was. But outwardly I tried to smile and thank those who greeted me. Ron, Don's tennis partner, was there too, and he stood behind me, gripping my shoulders.

No words accompanied his action, but he offered strength as well as sympathy. His touch said he wasn't expecting Don back at Maranatha next year either.

Then another friend patted my arm. "You and Don are such wonderful Christians. I just know God is going to heal him."

I couldn't answer as the tears ran down my cheeks. She didn't know us well after all. If Don's healing depended on *our* goodness, we had no hope.

Chapter Two

Everything's Normal?

August 15, 1981
Ann Arbor, Michigan

The following Saturday, we were at the University of Michigan Hospital in Ann Arbor. Jay and Holly would stay with my parents in nearby Chelsea.

That first afternoon, we met several doctors. Our resident was a pleasant young man who took the medical history, gave a thorough examination and then reminded us that U of M is a teaching institution. Thus, Don would be observed by students in various stages of training. We, of course, agreed to such an arrangement, but soon I began to dread those clinical rounds. Don was merely an interesting terminal case to many of the observers. I wanted to shake them as they read the charts or held up the latest CAT scans.

"Look at *him!*" I wanted to shout. "He's not just 'a 38-year-old, Caucasian male with multiple metastatic lesions to the brain. Malignant melanoma.' He's a good husband and daddy who tries to follow the Lord. He's a loyal U-M football fan! His favorite vacation day is golf in the morning and tennis in the afternoon. Look at him!"

Of course I never shouted those things, but I stared at the students, willing them to look at our faces. Don handled the same discomfort by speaking directly to them, sometimes asking a question, sometimes teasing the examiner about cold hands. Perhaps the students' distance actually was their emotional protection. Maybe most didn't know how to respond, so they hid behind their concept of "professionalism."

One of the students, though, smiled at us directly. We met Mr. Nelson that first afternoon Don checked in. He had asked for yet another case history, carefully explaining the necessity for the repeated questions and examinations, stressing the university's teaching status. He looked little older than many of our students, so we first asked him what high school he had attended. He answered enthusiastically, but then skillfully turned the conversation back to the medical history. Don stretched out and put his hands behind his head in preparation to answer the questions. That was the most relaxed he had been all day.

As Mr. Nelson asked when the headaches first started, the procedure used for the first operation, and which family members had also had cancer, I opened the canvas bag that I now carried constantly. Don grinned as I untangled more threads, so I held the Pharaoh up for him to see the progress.

Then as he answered Mr. Nelson's questions, I occasionally corrected him. "Honey, your grandma had cancer too. Remember? It was in the 1920s just after their visit back to Scotland." Or "Wait, Dale had kidney stones a couple of years ago."

Finally Mr. Nelson turned to me apologetically. "Mrs. Aldrich, it's important that *Mr.* Aldrich answer these questions. We need to see how much of his normal brain function has been impaired by the lesions."

Properly chastened, I gave a startled "I'm sorry" and turned back to the Pharaoh.

I believe the Lord has given us modern doctors and medicine. We'll follow their advice, but leave the outcome totally in the Lord's hands. He's in charge.

Don chuckled. "But this is 'normal brain function' for me," he said. "San's always kept track of the family news. She sends the birthday cards and, at weddings, reminds me which of my cousins are divorced, so I don't ask about the wrong spouse. If you want family history, you have to talk to her."

I smiled at my bearded Scotsman, grateful for this defense. But I bent over the needlepoint as Mr. Nelson continued the questions. The black border around the Pharaoh had given me trouble all summer, so I was anxious to finish it. Then just as I was ready to connect the sides, I realized I had miscounted the canvas spaces. Groan. It would do no good to pull out those hundreds of stitches; much of the background was already completed. Well, my choices were limited. I could abandon this whole project and go back to my quilting, or I could adjust the stitches and accept the obvious zig-zag that would result.

I glanced at Don as he answered questions. How appropriate that I discovered the mistake right then—with him in blue pajamas on top of a white hospital sheet. The

needlepoint imperfection was just a tiny reminder of what
we were facing in our personal lives. We could give up,
saying it was hopeless. Or we could make the necessary
adjustments and allow the Lord to create something beautiful out of this imperfect zig-zag in our lives. I touched the
black, broken line in the pattern and spoke to God in my
heart.

"This can still be beautiful, Lord—just as our remaining time can be. Create your beauty, Lord. I trust you to
bring your good out of this evil."

* * *

I left the hospital as late as possible that first night, but
kissed Don heartily, promising to be back early in the
morning.

Jay and Holly were already in bed by the time I arrived
at my parents' home. My mother, shorter than I and dark-
haired, asked about the doctor's plans. But my dad, a big
German, was unusually quiet. I gave them a review of the
day, but soon climbed the narrow stairs to my old room.
Mother knew I would want Jay and Holly near me, so she
had set up two cots across from the small iron bed that had
been mine before I married.

In the moonlit room, I sat on the edge of the bed, listening to the soft breathing of my children. The stately
pine trees planted before the turn of the century still
shielded the windows. The wallpaper was the same too. I
studied the lavender and blue flowers, remembering my
delight at the choice when our family moved in during my
senior year in high school.

Suddenly I covered my face with my hands, reluctant
to face the night back in my old room. The last time I had
slept in that room had been 15 years ago — the night

before Don and I were married. That night, in 1966, I'd had trouble getting to sleep as I wondered what it would be like to be a wife. Tonight I would wonder what it would be like to be a widow.

* * *

The rest of the week seemed as though we were walking through a bad dream. Countless doctors saw him, and dozens of our friends came to the hospital each day. Gradually the doctors were eliminating the things they could do for Don. They finally decided to try heavy radiation treatments, followed by massive dosages of standard chemotherapy. Solemn Doctor Silver, an oncologist, gave us the decision Wednesday afternoon. We would have a consultation with the radiologists that afternoon.

When we were alone again, Don was quiet. I held his hand to my face.

"Donnie, we don't have to stay here," I said. "I'll take you anyplace you want to go."

Then I told him about the calls from a friend who insisted I take Don to a special clinic in California where he would be treated with nutritional therapy. Another had given me the number of a doctor in Lexington who'd treated their friend.

Don shook his head. "Boy, you've had to put up with me all day and then have to handle calls like that at night? I hope you told them I have to be comfortable with whatever is done. I don't want to go that far from home. Besides, I believe the Lord has given us modern doctors and medicine. We'll follow their advice, but leave the outcome totally in the Lord's hands. He's in charge. He can be trusted with this."

He put his right arm over his eyes. "I'm anxious to

start whatever treatment they want me to have here. I'll do anything at all if it'll help me stay with my 'babies.' They need their goofy daddy."

I understood the impulse of family members to snatch up a patient and whisk him into some exotic clinic promising a cure. Before all this had happened, I'd shaken my head as I heard about people escaping into Mexico or kidnapping their children out of the hospital. But now the one thing keeping me from flying Don and the children to the other side of the world was Don's determination not to leave home. Whatever time was left, I wanted it to be good, not filled with horrible pain for him and wretched memories for us.

Soon, an attendant from the radiation department arrived to escort us downstairs for our consultation. Eyes straight ahead, neither one of us looked at the people waiting in the lobby for their turn beneath those mysterious machines sending Xrays into the body, killing both healthy and diseased cells.

The foreign doctor carefully explained the process and then stammered an apology. "This isn't a cure, you understand. We are just trying to help you . . . . "

He paused, searching for the right phrase. I finished it for him: "You're just helping us buy a little time."

He nodded, relieved I understood, and left to check on the availability of a machine. Don was to have the first of the 15 treatments immediately.

I'd wanted a miracle before all this started, but we weren't going to get a last-minute reprieve. Don gave me one of his "Well, here we are" looks. All my resolve to be strong for him faded in that moment and the tears rolled down my cheeks. He closed his eyes and whispered, "Don't cry. Please don't cry." My arms tightened around his shoulders.

At last a machine was available. We'd already been warned that Don's hair would fall out and his strength would be severely affected. We'd also received the almost casual warning that massive dosages could cause paralysis. The doctor had hastily assured us that such complications rarely happened, but the warning had to be given by law. It was that statement I remembered as I ran the water in the rest room sink, determined the others in the waiting room not hear my fearful sobs.

I leaned against the sink, splashing the cold water onto my face. Were we doing the right thing? What if the radiation made   things worse? The sobs were threatening to surface again, so I put my face directly under the running water, rebelling at this new weak creature I'd become. Then I put on the brave expression saved for public appearances, and went out into the waiting room, determined not to see the numerous hairs on the back of the chairs, nor the children wearing baseball caps to cover their bald heads.

* * *

As the week continued, the list of visitors grew. Mother brought Jay and Holly over each evening so they could give Don a good-night hug, but those little visits didn't fill that need of feeling like a family. We wanted to be home— together.

Don's family was with us often. And my brother, Mitch, and sisters Thea and Greta came from out of town too. The only one missing was my sister Nancy, who lived in Florida. We hadn't seen her for two years. After one exceptionally busy afternoon, Don made the comment that everyone in the tri-states had visited. Then he chuckled. "But I won't believe I'm really sick until Nancy shows up."

I returned his grin, but inwardly I was trying to sort

out the meaning behind his words. Wasn't he hearing the doctors when they answered his questions about the seriousness of his condition? Was it still a bad dream to him? I didn't get my answer until Friday afternoon. The day was a Michigan delight— blue sky, soft breezes and vibrant green maples. We escaped the stuffy hospital room. I hastily scribbled a note for the doctors but hoped no one would find us. I wanted time alone with Don.

Has there ever been a more beautiful day? Don walked out through the hospital door, his arm across my shoulders. It was a casual, loving gesture, but I felt him leaning heavily against me and I walked very slowly to the giant tree in the middle of the front lawn.

Don sprawled beside me, his head resting in my lap. I stroked his blond hair ever so gently, wondering how soon it would begin to fall out. Don appeared to be dozing under my hand, so I was startled when he spoke.

"San, we have some things we better talk about. Look, I know God can heal me if that's what He wants. But maybe He has other plans. If the doctors are right, then I've got to face up to not being here. And that means you've got decisions to make."

I cradled my arms across his shoulders and leaned forward to kiss his forehead, wanting to shield him from saying these things.

He continued. "I'd like you to ask your parents if they'd mind if I was buried in their family plot in Chelsea. I know there isn't room for me to be buried next to my mother in Flint. Besides, you won't be going up there that often."

Maybe he felt my stomach tighten in my determination to let him say whatever he needed to. But the thought of him lying cold and still beneath the dirt was too horrible to think about.

"San, I know I won't really be there. It's like the time your grandmother died and Jay told Holly the breathin' part was in heaven. But while I believe that, I can't really comprehend it. Maybe I want to do that for your mother as well as for you and the kiddos. She's helped fill the void my mom left and she's going to have a rough time when all this is over. Just don't let her spend a lot of time at the cemetery. And I don't want you down there all the time either."

I looked up at the mass of green leaves above us, blinking my eyes. This couldn't be happening!

He continued. "And I want you to know that you aren't to hide away when all this is over. My kiddos need a daddy."

My astonishment forced out the words. "Don! They need *their* daddy, not just *a* daddy. Don't make me listen to this!"

He shook his head. "No, San. You know the standing joke if the situation were reversed. As much as I want you to continue with your writing, I don't want you hiding behind that desk. It's a big world out there. I want you to be part of it."

I knew the joke all right. I'd always teased him about how soon he would remarry if anything happened to me. I'd even added that he'd double date to my funeral. Suddenly none of this was funny at all.

He was waiting for a response. "Donnie," I stammered, "the thought of anyone else in our lives is too overwhelming."

"OK, just remember what I said. And another thing—I know the Lord is going to give you a ministry out of this."

His voice trailed off. I gently continued to stroke his forehead, but I didn't want a "ministry." I wanted him.

* * *

That night when I asked my parents about the family grave plot, they were silent for several minutes. I didn't look at them for fear I'd cry again, but I could hear stifled little sobs from Mother. Finally Dad spoke.

"We have seven empty plots over there—all saved for family. Don's family. Of course he can be buried there."

Again the heavy silence filled the room. I could hear Jay and Holly's chatter as my sister Greta supervised them as they popped corn in the kitchen. I picked at a rough cuticle, wondering when I'd ever have time, or the energy, to do my nails again.

"I don't want you thinking I'm planning for Don to die soon," I said. "It's just that he wanted me to ask you, so I did. Hundreds of people are praying for him. In spite of my worry, I honestly feel he's going to get better. We may have some dark days ahead yet, but he *will* get better. You can't have that many people praying and not get results."

Mother, our prayer warrior, nodded. Dad's German jaw was set. "I've been checking up on this type of brain cancer," he said. "You'll be praying for him to die before this is over!"

My heart sent up an arrow prayer, asking for the right illustration for my mechanic father. "Dad, God made Don. He can repair him, too, if that's part of His plan."

Suddenly Dad smiled, the first I'd seen since Don had gotten sick. "Well, I guess that's right. It's a pretty poor mechanic who can't repair his own machine."

* * *

When I arrived at the hospital the next morning, Don was

lying on top of the bedspread, his arm across his eyes, and his Bible open on his chest. I rubbed his toes to let him know I was there. He smiled when he saw me, but it was one of relief rather than happiness. He asked his usual questions about Jay and Holly, and who had called from Maranatha, but he wasn't really listening to my answers. Finally he looked directly at me.

> *"Dad, God made Don. He can repair him, too, if that's part of His plan"* . . . *"Well, I guess that's right. It's a pretty poor mechanic who can't repair his own machine."*

"Did you ask your folks?"

He was thinking of the cemetery. "Yes," I answered. "Of course they agreed. Look, do you want to go outside? It's awfully stuffy in here today."

He shook his head. "No. I don't feel like doing anything. I'm bummed today, San. I'm glad you're here with me, but I don't want to talk. Okay?"

I leaned over to kiss his forehead. "You have every right to be bummed. Want me to read some of the cheerful Psalms?"

He nodded. "Start with the Twenty-third Psalm. If anything's going to help, that one will. Ah, San, I don't want to be bummed. I want so much to be a good warrior in all of this. I want so much for others to see the reality of God's comfort."

He closed his eyes and I began to read. My voice faltered at "the valley of the shadow of death." I looked at Don. His eyes were still closed. "Go on," he said.

I couldn't bite my lip and read at the same time, so I

continued to falter. At the last verse, Don whispered the words: "And I will dwell in the house of the Lord *forever.*"

* * *

The next morning I arrived at the hospital early; Don's quietness worried me. I stepped into his room, my most determined smile neatly in place. His bed was empty!

As I stepped back into the hall, I saw the announcement for chapel on the eighth floor. That's where he'd go, surely.

The services had already begun by the time I arrived at the chapel. I stood in the back, looking at each head as I searched for that familiar blond hair. He wasn't there. Disappointed, I started to leave. But the minister asked the group to recite the Twenty-third Psalm. As the familiar words came, I looked at the group. Many were in bathrobes. Some sat next to weary family members. Others sadly sat alone.

They were approaching the phrase "valley of the shadow of death" now. How many of them faltered at those words? Was it real to them too? I continued to stare at the backs of their heads. So many hurts. What about that young woman over there, sitting alone? Or that old man with his wheelchair pulled close to the pew where his white-haired wife sat? And that little bald kid between his parents. What awful things were they facing?

I turned away, determined to find Don. We were not the only hurting people.

* * *

Perhaps my worry wouldn't have been so great if Don hadn't been so despondent yesterday. Think. Where would he be on a beautiful day? *Lord, please help.* Suddenly I had the impulse to go to the tennis courts I noticed yesterday behind nearby apartments.

Just as I crossed the street, I spotted the familiar dark blue bathrobe. Don was walking slowly, his hands clasped behind his back. I hurried to catch up to him.

He wasn't surprised I'd found him. "I knew you'd know where to look," he said. "I'm glad you're here."

I took his arm to give him something to lean on. "How you feeling today, Donnie?"

He motioned for us to sit on the grassy bank above the tennis courts. "I'm still not thrilled with this whole business," he said. "But I'm not bummed. I tried that yesterday and made myself feel worse. It's like we read yesterday—God is with us in this mess. I've just got to keep reminding myself of that."

Then his familiar, teasing grin appeared. "So don't get too excited about what I said the other day about your getting a new man. I'm going to do all I can to make sure you're stuck with the old one for a while longer."

I leaned against his shoulder, relieved at the change. We sat quietly for several minutes, just watching the players on the courts below us. Occasionally Don, forever the coach, would mutter a "Not a lob, you dummy. Hit to his backhand."

Suddenly he turned back to me. "See that? With God's help, I'm going to play tennis again."

That afternoon, Dr. Silver brought us the welcomed news that Don could go home after the next day's radiation treatment and continue as an outpatient. The chemotherapy would begin the following week—also in the outpatient clinic, if we preferred. We didn't have to discuss that one. We wanted to be home. We wanted to be a family again.

* * *

It was wonderful to be home again, but the days were hectic. Each morning Don had radiation, followed by visits from friends. And always I tried to think of creative, healthy foods that Don would enjoy. But each day the scale showed another pound lost.

Don also was having trouble sleeping. In addition to bizarre dreams, he couldn't lie on his left side because of a strange soreness. It started just beneath his shoulder blade and curved around to the top of his stomach. When the little blisters appeared, we decided it had to be a radiation rash (whatever that was) and showed them to the nurse when we arrived for Friday morning's treatment.

She studied the skin, making pitying sounds with her mouth. I wanted to comment that the first thing they were supposed to have learned in medical training was never to say "oops," but I wasn't sure she'd appreciate the remark. Finally she called the doctor in to see the blisters. He too shook his head and made the same sad sounds.

"Well?" I tried to keep the panic out of my voice. "Is it a radiation rash?"

They both shook their heads. "No," the nurse said, "that's nothing from us. We didn't do that."

I glanced at Don as he made one of his wide-eyed clown faces as she stressed their innocence.

"Then what is it?" I was tired of this nonsense.

The foreign doctor mumbled something about "herpes zoster" and turned to his nurse. "What do you call it here?"

"Shingles," she said simply.

Shingles? Don and I looked at one another. His grandmother's heart had been weakened by the severe case she'd had, and she had died within two weeks of their appearance. How I wish we hadn't known that.

The nurse saw the look that we exchanged. "Shingles aren't so bad," she said. "They'll hurt for a couple of weeks and then clear up. It's an inflammation of the nerve endings. These blisters are exposing the nerves, that's why they hurt so. It's like having adult chicken pox. Just take baking soda baths and try to rest. There's nothing to do for them except wait for them to run their course."

Trusting soul that I used to be, I believed her.

* * *

The next radiation wasn't scheduled until Monday, so Don wanted to go back to Maranatha for the weekend. He even insisted upon taking his golf clubs, saying he wanted to go out "one more time with the guys." He quickly added, "Once more *this* year," but I'd caught the implication. Of course we'd go. Besides, I didn't want to argue about a trip just before I told him about my decision to quit teaching.

Once he was safely settled in his comfortable orange chair in our family room, I poured iced tea and positioned a pillow next to his sore side. Then I made my announcement.

"Don, I've decided not to go back to teaching next week. I'm taking a personal leave."

He never looked up. "Don't be silly. Of course you're going back."

"No, I'm not! I'm going to stay home and take care of you."

Then thinking I had a fool-proof argument I added, "Then when you nap in the afternoon, I'll finish Marta's book."

I couldn't read the look in his eyes. Was it exasperation? Finally he spoke. "Ah, San, how do I explain this? I need to know everything's normal. I need to know you and Jay and Holly do normal things even if I can't. We aren't going to discuss it anymore. I want a normal household."

Normal? Our whole world had suddenly gone crazy, and he's insisting upon business as usual? I stared at him. How could he run our home, and me, with just two words: "Ah, San." I was tempted to start a good fight, but his blue eyes urged me not to. I could do nothing but pack the car for Maranatha.

* * *

I drove the three hours to Muskegon, but just before we turned onto Lake Harbor Road, Don asked me to pull over and let him drive onto the conference grounds. I didn't even bother to ask why. It was his need to appear "normal."

As we pulled into the drive, his voice was soft. "Two weeks ago I wondered if I'd ever see that hill again. There it is—and it's never looked so good."

I nodded. Some of the leaves on the maples were starting to change color for the coming autumn, but nothing else was different. How could Maranatha appear so unchanged when nothing ever again would be the same?

A "Welcome Aldrichs" sign was on the front of our place and fruit and flowers on the kitchen counter. I was delighted by the tangible expressions of love, but found myself warning would-be huggers of Don's tender side. I didn't care if they thought I was a mother hen; I'd seen him grimace with those hugs.

Morrie and his other golfing buddies had enthusiastically agreed to Don's plans to join their usual Saturday morning game. Even though he would be renting a cart, I worried. I mumbled about his "not over-doing," but he ignored it. If all these activities that he called "normal" were part of his denial of the situation, then he had to work through them at his own pace. Based upon their available data, the doctors had handed him a death sentence. He needed time to sort out the awful reality.

The next morning, Jay and Holly and I packed away dishes and linens for the winter. I wanted to have everything finished before the golfers' annual luncheon that afternoon. The lunch had been delayed two weeks in Don's behalf, so special excitement was in that day's preparations. Morrie's wife, Gert, sympathized with both my determination to alter our red meat diet and with Don's frustration over his loss of taste. She prepared a hearty Dutch chicken soup instead of the usual potato salad and ham.

A solemn aura hung over the group as they ate. Normally friendly banter flew as they teased each other about missed putts and sand traps, but all of that was missing. Even the trophy awards were formal presentations.

* * *

During the next week my aunt and, later, two of our friends came to pray and anoint Don with oil. That was a new idea to us, but since it was in the book of James, we submitted to it—even welcomed it. Others might have accused us of clutching at straws, but we were determined not to leave one stone unturned in our search for healing.

By then, Don's hair was falling out. It was depressing to find the great handfuls of blond strands upon his pillow every morning. More came out with each bath, plugging the drain, clinging to the towel. Don had said at the first sign of "fall-out" he'd just have his head shaved and be another Yul Brynner. When the radiologist heard of his plans, he insisted Don had to wait until after the treatments in case the skin should be nicked. Radiation to an open sore would cause extreme problems, he said. Extreme problems? Did he mean the things we were already facing were nothing? I didn't want to know.

Wednesday morning Jay and Holly's school started before either one of our high schools did. That was also the big day for the first chemotherapy. Don's brothers, Dale and Doug, his dad and stepmother insisted upon going with him for the first treatment. As much as I wanted to be with him, I knew they needed to be involved too. Besides, other treatments would follow. Don needed his Flint family right now, and Jay and Holly needed me.

Even with all of the things I had to do, the afternoon was very long. Of course, I didn't get any typing accomplished; I kept listening for a car in the drive. When at last they arrived, I ran to greet my man.

His face was pale as he barely nodded at me on his way to his favorite chair. Dale and Doug supplied me with the details. Yes, he'd thrown up on the way home. No, he probably wouldn't feel like eating for a while, especially since the chemotherapy would undoubtedly cause sores in his mouth after a couple of days. We were to watch for that.

Even as we talked, Don's stomach was threatening him again. Our neighbor Bill had offered him wine if he ever needed it, so I called. I'm opposed to alcohol, but if a glass of wine would settle Don's stomach, I'd even start buying it. That was a milestone decision for me, and I didn't even flinch.

Some of my former students had heard about the

impending chemotherapy and timidly offered to supply us with marijuana in order to help calm the nausea. They had even apologized as they offered, knowing our stand against drugs. But while Don had flatly refused the relayed offer, I was horrified to discover I had tucked the information into the back of my mind just in case we needed it in the future. Me? The self-righteous Pharisee who had once condemned all smokers?

I don't know what bothered me most—discovering I was suddenly part of the situation ethics crowd, or knowing I would accept anything that would help make the treatments bearable. My prayer that night was filled with much soul-searching. Why did everything have to be a battle with me? Why couldn't I just relax and let the Lord do everything? Where was the line between praying as though everything depended on Him, and yet working as though everything depended on me? All of the simple mores I'd lived by for so long were suddenly full of complicated twists.

"Lord," I prayed, "I do trust your goodness, but I'm a doer too. Don't let me do anything to harm your name though. . . ." I paused several moments before I could add, "No matter what." I knew then we'd never accept the illegal drug offers coming our way. But another chink of my Pharisee armor fell away.

* * *

The rest of that week was lost in busy days and long nights. Don's shingles were worsening; several spots were starting to ulcerate. None of our doctors at the hospital could offer anything for them, saying they'd just have to run their course. I wish we'd known to have him take vitamin B internally and to squeeze the oil from a vitamin E capsule onto the blisters. Maybe we could have stopped the terrible pain caused by the exposed nerve endings.

Neither one of us could remember what it had been like to sleep through the night. I hadn't been this tired since both children were babies. How was I going to teach this year if I couldn't sleep at night?

Jay and Holly were already settled into their Christian school; Jay in the third grade and Holly in the second. I'd talked with both of their teachers, explaining the problem, and was surprised to hear that the entire staff already knew about our situation and had begun praying. Their attitude encouraged me greatly.

On the day after Labor Day both Don's and my high schools had staff meetings. After analyzing my morning schedule, the alarm was set for five o'clock. That way I could have a few quiet moments alone with the Lord, take care of my grooming, and still have time to help Don with his morning baking soda bath. His legs weren't strong, and I worried about his attempting to take a bath alone.

But on staff day, Don startled me by insisting he was going to his school. His explanation was a simple, "I want to show them I'm not dead yet!"

I looked at his patchy hair and thinning frame and wasn't so sure his fellow teachers would be encouraged to see him. But it was something he needed to do. Besides, his two best friends would be there with him. It was useless to argue.

His report that night was positive. He'd been greeted by his fellow-workers and even thumped occasionally on the back. I grimaced at the thought of the pain that must have caused. Then he surprised me with another decision.

"I'm going to ask Dr. Silver when I can go back part-time. There's no reason why I can't teach a couple of hours each day, just to keep my hand in until I go back full time."

I stared back at him, wondering how his waning strength would allow him to get through even two hours of high school business law and accounting.

"Don, you said your substitute is capable. Let's just concentrate upon your getting well first, then we'll talk about the classroom."

I was having trouble thinking that far ahead since the doctors had warned me the crisis would undoubtedly come in September. Why, that was this month! This was starting to get even more complicated—what was reality and what was lack of faith on my part? What was denial and what was true faith in Don's attitude?

While these questions ricocheted inside me, Don stared at me. Then he announced, "I *will* go back to teaching!"

He certainly wasn't worried about the money, because his salary would continue under his sick-leave clause. It was something stronger than that. I watched him ease down into his orange chair. Well, if positive attitude was the key in even "hopeless" cases, he was off to a great start.

My own staff meeting that day had been interesting, too. Even though I was frustrated at having to be there, it was good to be back. Carl Amann, a close friend from church, had already told many of our co-workers about Don's trauma, and they stopped by my room to express sorrow. Even the awkwardly stammered words encouraged me. It was good to know so many people cared.

After the typical first-day-of-new-year meeting, the new principal, Mark Gutman, announced I was to take off whatever time I needed.

I thanked him. "I appreciate your kindness, but while I'm here teaching, my students will have 100 percent from me. When I can't give that, I won't be in. Fair enough?"

He looked surprised. Perhaps he thought I'd gush gratitude or perhaps merely nod my head and bite my lip. But I'd always said the classroom was no place for personal problems. It made no difference now that it was *my* life in turmoil. I had students to prepare for college.

After our staff meeting, I walked down to room 152 and opened the door. Once called the "dungeon" because of its depressing color, my previous classical mythology students had transformed it into a daydreamer's delight. The front and side walls had scenes and characters from Roman, Greek and Norse mythologies. Hercules strangling the serpents, Athena and her shield, Pegasus springing from the blood of the Gorgon, and other scenes brightened the once grimy wall facing the door. My favorite picture was at the top. It was of a Greek man with arms outstretched toward the face of his god. I used it to illustrate my definition of mythology on each opening day.

"Mythology is ancient man reaching up to his god," I'd say. "But Christianity is God reaching down to man through His Son, Jesus."

The faces of the Christian students would immediately brighten. And in all those years of teaching, only one student challenged me for presenting "religion." I had chuckled.

"Look," I said, "if they insist I teach the Indian myth of the world growing from a piece of magic moss tossed on the back of Great Turtle, I can certainly include what I know is true."

Now after the staff meeting, I studied those marvelous walls. Maybe Don was right: it would be good to do something normal. At least here I could control my environment.

* * *

The best part of those first few weeks of school was the special attention Don received from his friends. His buddies, Bill Fife and John Vladu, not only kept him informed about the staff, but came over to watch football games with him. To hear them laugh together after a "dumb" play was especially delightful to me. In the past, I'd been irritated by what I saw as wasted time. Now I was thankful for anything that kept Don busy. He was becoming increasingly frustrated by watching me do all of the work since he couldn't help. Too, we seemed to be waiting for the big crisis the doctors had warned about. But so far everything was continuing in the hectic pace of everyday coping.

One morning I was especially rushed. Don's bath had taken extra time because of the new sores on his side. Then Jay couldn't find a book. One thing after another went wrong before the children and I could get out the door.

The first class started at 7:30 A.M., and the new principal left warning memos in the mailboxes of teachers arriving after 7:15. I didn't want him to think I was taking undue advantage of his concern for my home situation at the beginning of the year.

Another red light stopped me; I could feel my heart thumping with impatience. "Lord, help!" Immediately the thought came I was to concentrate upon all of the good things.

Good things? Well, I could be thankful the situation wasn't worse; at least Don was still with us and functioning. He had refused my offer to have a nurse stay with him, saying he'd save that for when he needed it. I was thankful Jay and Holly had wonderful teachers who were concerned about the pressures they were experiencing. And I could certainly be thankful I was on my way to spend the day with delightful students. My list continued. By the time I arrived at my school, I was calm.

But the next morning brought another problem. Since it was early September, the humidity was especially high. I insisted on fixing Holly's hair in a ponytail because I didn't have time to fuss with it and put in into the bun or pigtails she usually liked. But with it pulled straight back, it was too stark for her little face. She began to cry, saying the kids would say she looked "stupid." I was tempted to give in and redo it, but Don shook his head at me. Instead he prayed aloud for her, asking that she be able to ignore any comments and that, in fact, the other children would be kind. She blew her nose but said no more about the ponytail.

On the way to school that morning, I thought about Don's prayer solution. Actually, we'd gotten along perfectly since the crisis began. I was taking good care of him, even waiting on him in a way I'd sworn never to do for any man. (My excuse was I'd seen too much servitude among the women in my Southern culture.) Meanwhile, Don was quick to seek a prayerful solution for our daily lives, and he no longer made sarcastic comments that so quickly pierced my shaky ego. With tears running down my cheeks, I realized it had taken this crisis to cause us to treat each other the way we had wanted for the past 15 years.

CHAPTER THREE

Don't You Care, God?

October 7, 1981
Canton, Michigan

With so many people praying for Don, we were convinced the CAT scan scheduled for early October would show improvement. Meanwhile, the chemotherapy dosage increased.

Our Tennessean friend, Randall Taylor, insisted upon taking Don for chemo every third Wednesday. Then I took two days off from work to care for my Scotsman. Even though the treatments were severe, the increasing pain from the shingles was the most frustrating. Several areas below his shoulder blade had ulcerated into something called "post herpic neuralgia." Whatever they labeled it, it wasn't clearing as the nurse had promised.

Each morning after the chemotherapy, my mother called to remind Don of her constant prayers. After they'd talk, he'd say, "I've got the best mother-in-law in the world." I tried not to be irritated at the others he would have liked to have heard from too. Instead I wondered how many times I had missed encouraging someone in that same way.

Then in the first week of October, Randall's Nashville sister-in-law, Jean Taylor, sent Don a card ending with, "I think it stinks you have shingles on top of everything else!" Don and I laughed aloud. We knew it stunk too, but thought it was unchristian to voice that. Constantly I struggled with what my proper attitude should be. I wanted so much for others to see God's reality and His comfort even in the midst of trauma, but a woman in our Bible study accused us of spiritual pride.

"Well, I'm not surprised you're having all this trouble," she cooed piously. "Both you and Don have been saying, 'Look what the Lord is doing for us.'"

On top of everything else, I didn't need to argue my many sins. I tiredly remarked about the thin line between offering praise for our heavenly Father's help and displaying pride, but she remained convinced we were being punished. *Spiritual* pride was the last thing I had ever expected to be accused of.

Then that week's CAT scan further disappointed us— the cancer was still very much there. Dr. Silver stressed that the lesions hadn't grown, but I wanted them to be *gone!* Hadn't Don been prayed over and for? Weren't we trying to do everything we possibly could—limiting red meats, increasing whole grains, taking a handful of vitamins each day? Yet nothing was working.

He couldn't even enjoy the beautiful autumn that people said we were having. I saw it only to or from school, but I longed to be outside with our usual activities—cider mills, antique shows and walks in the woods. But all of us were housebound.

Late one afternoon I stood at the front door, my arms filled with laundry, just as the husband across the street bounded into his car, tennis racket in hand. Jealousy seized me. Then I remembered the magazine story of a cat close to death after being hit by a car. The parents wanted their son to accept the cat's fate, but he insisted upon praying. The cat got well. Now my anger tumbled out.

If I'd trusted [God] during the happy times, I had to trust Him in the valley. But one thing was still in my control—I could insist we all go to the park.

"OK, God, so why did you heal that cat, and not Don?"

I didn't expect an answer, I just wanted to let God know I thought the whole thing was stinky—and not just the shingles. I listed all of the frustrations of the past few weeks, ending with not being able to be outside on such a beautiful day.

When I finally paused for breath, I waited, almost daring Him to answer. But instead of a rebuttal came peace— as though Someone was saying, "I *am* here."

That wasn't the answer I wanted, but if I believed God was sovereign, I had to accept it. If I'd trusted Him during the happy times, I had to trust Him in the valley. But one thing was still in my control—I could insist we all go to the park.

Jay and Holly squealed at my plans for a picnic, but Don balked. It was only when he saw their disappointment that he set his jaw and pulled himself out of his orange chair. "I guess I can be as uncomfortable there as I am here."

At the park, Jay and Holly sprinted for the swings. I

didn't want Don watching healthy bodies on the soccer field so I motioned toward the path leading to a stand of trees. He leaned heavily against me as he eased to the ground beneath the largest tree. We could hear the excited calls from the soccer game.

His head was down; he was undoubtedly hearing those same happy sounds. I wanted to call him back to me. "Don, look! We're sitting under a hickory tree. I haven't seen one in years. When I was a kid, we used to gather the nuts for the fudge Mother made on snowy evenings."

I spotted empty hulls in the short grass. "I guess the squirrels beat us to them this year. We'll have to remember to come here early next year."

He glanced at me when I said "next year," but made no comment. He'd had rough days before, but at least he'd been able to talk through some of his turmoil. Why hadn't I grabbed my Bible before we came here? Reading the Psalms always helped both of us. David had expressed his own heart, surely never dreaming his words would encourage countless readers. I'd wanted our experience to bring some glory to our Father, too, but we were sitting miserably under a hickory tree. Wouldn't the Lord be better glorified through Don's healing? Maybe I better tackle this issue head-on. I tried again.

"Donnie, I'm bummed. Please talk to me. I'm upset God hasn't healed you *our* way. I'm angry the CAT scan showed the same old lesions. I wanted this to be a testimony to God's healing power. But He's doing it His way, not mine, and I'm struggling with that."

The soccer crowd was cheering again. Don gestured that he wanted to stand up. "I know, San. I don't try to make sense out of this anymore. I know one thing, though; I've got to get back to teaching. This sitting around counting the minutes is making me stir-crazy. I'm going to stop asking the Lord to take away this pain. I'm just going to ask Him to help me bear it."

* * *

The decision Don made that day showed immediately. He rested for a while when we returned home, but soon called one of his friends, asking to be picked up for their school's football game that night. He'd always worked in the press box, and I worried he'd be depressed when he saw someone else doing his job. But I shook off my uneasiness and kissed him good-bye; he had to get out more.

But at 7:30, my stomach tightened. Something was wrong. I stood by the sink, my heart pounding. Then the phone rang.

Don had stumbled and gashed his leg, his boss said. *I knew it! Why hadn't I insisted he use a cane?* While I chastened myself for not having taken better care of Don, his boss said they'd taken him by ambulance to Wayne County Hospital. Did I know how to get there? Could they do anything for me?

I wanted to yell, "Yes! You can drive me there!" But I displayed that same calm I used when talking with the doctors: I assured him I'd be fine and that I'd leave immediately.

After a quick call to our neighborhood sitter, I pulled my jacket out of the closet just as the phone rang again. Quickly, I grabbed it, thinking it might be the doctor. But it was Gary Batherson, Don's friend from our Bible study. He cheerfully asked how I was, but I hastily cut him off, explaining Don's cut and my departure.

His voice was firm. "No way. I'm coming to get you." Before I could respond, he hung up.

For several moments, I stood with the phone receiver

still in my hand. Again the Lord had supplied the answer to my need, even though I had refused to ask.

Gary was the last one I would have thought of to help me. At the Bible studies I found his flippant manner irritating, especially when he was telling me to "loosen up." Our personalities simply clashed. When I'd complained to Don about Gary's Ph.D. in psychology surfacing, he'd laughed.

"Face it, San, you hate it when people try to figure you out. Why not be nice to him? Don't be afraid to let him see why I love you so much."

But the friction had continued right until his phone call. Minutes later, when he pulled into our drive, my first comment was a relieved, "Am I ever glad to see you." The Lord was healing in ways I hadn't expected.

At the hospital, Don was lying on a gurney, waiting for the numbing shots to take effect. "Boy, what a dummy I am, huh?" he said. "I can't even walk up steps without cutting my leg."

The cut was in fact two deep gashes. The doctor estimated it would take 50 stitches to close them. As we stood in the hall, Gary was intrigued by the people and ambulances arriving every few minutes. I ignored everything, even the young woman with the rope burns on her neck, and the teenage boy who'd tried to slash his wrists. Their attempts at suicide were undoubtedly cries for help, but how could they choose death while Don was trying so very hard to choose life?

* * *

As October passed, Don regained his sense of taste. To hear him say, "Great meal, San" became my daily goal. That remark never came after the brown rice casseroles, but at least he complained less about them. During those weeks his sexual strength also returned. When he had first arrived home from the hospital, we had been too worried about the general trauma to be concerned about the disruption of our good relationship. We had missed that closeness. Now that it was possible again, it became a celebration of life itself.

His side pain continued, but he'd nicknamed it "the little man with the pitchfork" because of the sharp jabs that came at regular intervals. We were hopeful again. One afternoon when I returned from school, I knew from the smug look on his face he'd been up to something. He'd visited his high school to tell his boss he wanted to return to teaching part-time!

I was astounded. How could he handle a classroom?

He saw the worry in my eyes. "Ah, come on, San. It isn't as though I'm doing construction work or teaching junior high. Business students are serious about their work. Besides, I'll be teaching just two classes a day. I've already checked with Dr. Silver. He said because of my progress, he'll give me a letter of return. He agrees it's a good idea to keep me busy."

I tried one more angle. "What about driving? You know he warned you could have a seizure."

My clown was no longer grinning. As he rubbed his tender side, he nodded. "I know. But that was when they expected me to die. I've asked God to prevent that, but if it's part of His plan, then to please protect innocent people. Look, I know this sounds funny, but as I prayed, His peace was all around me. I'm not going to have a seizure in the car, and nobody's going to be hurt."

Don had always made everything sound all right—whether it was convincing me to marry him while we were still in college or telling me I wasn't going to quit teaching. That was the end of the discussion. I shrugged, choosing to concentrate on Don's Maranatha board meeting that weekend in Grand Rapids.

Don was especially looking forward to the Saturday breakfast Dennis DeVries and his wife, Phyllis, had planned for us. I wondered how everyone would react to this new Don—bald, beardless and using a cane. Jay and Holly and I had time to get used to the gradual changes, but those who would be seeing him for the first time since the end of August would be shocked.

I needn't have worried. Even those who were momentarily taken aback recovered quickly and greeted us warmly. Morrie's fatherly hug enveloped us both, easing the comment one of the nurses in our group had just made.

She said Don was a walking miracle, so I know she meant to encourage me. Still I wish she hadn't added the rest of her story—one of her patients had been diagnosed two months ago with the same cancer as Don's and now was paralyzed and blind. I shuddered at her news. But already I had learned the present had enough problems; it would do no good to worry about the future.

* * *

Even though Don's return to the classroom left him exhausted each day, I admitted his joy outweighed my worry. How his eyes shone as he told me about his students. Unfortunately, *my* days in the classroom weren't going as well. I'd determined to keep my personal life from affecting teaching, but I was standing on the edge of a frightening abyss, trying to hang onto the Lord. I needed less pressure and a full night's sleep.

The problem peaked when I snapped at my assistant

principal after receiving a memo saying I hadn't turned in the previous day's attendance. Don's chemotherapy reaction had kept me home; it was a *substitute* teacher who hadn't turned in the attendance. I was "loaded for bear" when I marched into his office. I told him exactly what I thought of their record keeping and marched out—just as my head principal strolled in. Their astonished expressions let me know I'd made an impression all right. But it wasn't the one I'd wanted.

As I walked down the hall, I bit my lip to keep from crying. I had wanted to be a good witness in all of this, but I'd just yelled at my boss. Boy, some shining example of Christianity.

Just as I decided I'd have to apologize—as soon as I could talk, the head secretary, Vicki Brusinski, caught up to me. Always the dear office mom, she started to put her arms around me. If she did, I'd lose what little strength was left.

"Please don't," I said. "It'll be all right. I'm just so very tired. Maybe if I go wash my face. . . ."

The tears were going to splash onto my face. I quickly walked away from someone who wanted only to comfort me.

The next morning, I left for school in a dense late-autumn fog. Everything was so murky I had to drive by instinct on the back road. After several moments of the car's crawling pace, I knew the stop sign should be just ahead. Ah, there it was.

As the car edged forward, I decided the fog wouldn't be as dense on top of the overpass. At least I'd be able to see from there. I inched to the top, expecting only greater visibility. Instead I was treated to an incredible sight. The little valleys surrounding the expressway were filled with pink mist rather than depressing, murky fog. And above the mysterious haze were the sun's rays, showing through purple and orange clouds.

The cars on the road below crept through the murk I had just escaped. If only they could have this view!

When I had to leave the overpass and descend into the fog again, the memory of the beautiful scene went with me. I continued to school, strangely refreshed. Beauty would come after our personal fog too. I just hadn't made it to a place where I could see above it.

That afternoon I took a class to the library. When everyone was settled with their term-paper materials, I meandered from shelf to shelf, wishing I could read for pleasure. I thumbed through historical volumes, pausing at pioneer women's stories.

Their courage impressed me. But they had tackled each challenge without awareness of its future significance. They merely were trying to survive. My maternal grandmother, Mama Farley, used to say, "There are some things that all you can do with them is bear them!" It was time for me to show a little of that Kentucky fighting spirit.

* * *

Throughout that autumn, Don continued to prod me about Marta's book, so I typed each evening after everyone was in bed. I also worked on the Pharaoh whenever I could, trying to redeem every precious moment.

Thanksgiving was still two weeks away when I took a roll of film to nearby Novi for processing. I'd been there only in the spring, but now that the leaves were down, I could see a cemetery to the left. I'd always been interested in old tombstones, so I wandered over. As I stepped past the pines, I suddenly had the eerie feeling I'd seen this place before. Perhaps in a dream?

Straight ahead was a small limestone marker. Startled, I whispered the name: "Sarah, wife of Daniel Aldrich."

In the twilight, I could see only the partial date from the late 1800s. I looked around me, startled to see that most of the stones bore the Aldrich name! Weeks later I'd learn I'd been in Novi's Aldrich/Knapp cemetery. But on that day, I wondered only about those wives who had stood by their husbands' fresh graves. Did they have small children? Were they able to keep their farms? Or did the death of their husbands mean a double loss?

I stood there—an Aldrich of 1981—among the graves of century old Aldrichs and felt a kinship deeper than our common name. I wasn't the first woman—nor would I be the last—who had to watch the suffering of someone she loved and wonder about a future without him. My Kentucky grandmother had said, "None of us was put here to stay." But I'd lost sight of that universal truth until this crisis.

The next week, my sister Nancy called from Florida to say she planned to join us for Thanksgiving. Her husband had to work, but at least we'd get to see Nancy and 2-year-old Rachel. I couldn't wait to tell Don.

He grinned. "Well, it's like I said in the hospital. If Nancy's coming, I know I'm sick."

My three sisters and one brother would be together with our parents for the first time in years. I wanted everyone at our house, so Don could rest whenever he needed. Normally I would have set an extended table with all of the holiday finery. But we were analyzing and adjusting so many areas of our lives because of Don's illness that it was easy to transfer it to a large gathering too. I planned for three small tables, set with the everyday dishes, in front of the fireplace.

When I picked up Nancy and Rachel from the airport, a

Michigan wind pushed us across the parking lot. Winter had set in, and I hadn't noticed. On the expressway, I answered Nancy's questions about the treatments, but tried to sound positive. Don was looking forward to her visit; I didn't want it clouded by pessimism. But when I mentioned his appearance, she nodded.

"I know. I've already been warned."

Warned? Someone undoubtedly had told her if she wanted to see Don alive she'd better come now. I wanted to ease that tension.

"But don't worry; he's actually doing very well," I said. "He'll be in bed by the time we get home, but that's from the shingles mostly. Lots of things are getting back to normal."

To illustrate my point, I told about the argument we'd had just the week before over his purchase of a kerosene heater. But my comments lacked zest. Cancer certainly had taken the humor out of a good argument.

Thanksgiving that year was delightful. Never had the 15 family members gotten along so well. And that same attitude reigned whenever we were with Don's folks. It had taken a crisis to make us all set aside the unimportant issues.

* * *

Two days after Nancy and Rachel left, I finished Marta's book. As I pulled that last page out of the typewriter, I yelled a "wahoo" that surely rattled the windows.

The next morning at school, an office aide delivered a bouquet of fresh flowers to my classroom. My principal was right behind her, wondering who sent flowers to one of his teachers.

I held out the card which read, "Congratulations! You finished! Love, Hubby."

Briefly I explained. My astonished boss nodded. "You've got quite a guy there," he said. "I hope you hang on to him."

Quietly I answered, "Yes, I hope so too."

* * *

In the process of trying to hang onto Don, I was frustrated by his increasing shingles pain. We'd tried everything we knew— including vitamins and rest—but we weren't getting any help from the doctors. Finally we connected with Dr. Jung, a Toledo doctor, who tried acupuncture. We were especially impressed that he had asked if he could pray with us first, committing everything to the Lord— the Great Physician. We were delighted to have God's powers acknowledged by a doctor.

Unfortunately, even after the tenth treatment, the pain never fully cleared. But at least it eased enough to allow Don to join us for a few hours each evening instead of going to bed as soon as he came in from school. If nothing else, the acupuncture allowed us to feel like a family again.

Just before Christmas, Randall took Don for his chemotherapy again. Those appointments took all afternoon as they waited to see the doctor, waited for the blood count results and waited for an available chair in the treatment room.

Randall had to be out of town that afternoon, but insisted he was going to take Don to the hospital for all the waiting. I could arrive during the actual treatment and then take him home.

Jay and Holly went with me to pick up their dad. I knew Don's chemotherapy was administered intravenously, but

I'd never thought to tell the kiddos that. As soon as we arrived, we saw Don sitting in a comfortable chair, his hand on an IV board, and the double vial of pale liquid dripping into the connecting tube.

Holly immediately cooed another, "Oh, poor Daddy," as she studied the needle in the back of his hand. But Jay's whispered comment was filled with relief. "Is that all it is?"

Poor little guy. What terrible machine had his mind created that caused his dad to be so sick? No longer would I assume they didn't have questions just because they didn't ask.

* * *

Christmas had a special glow that year as we visted relatives and entertained friends. But hanging over us was the awareness that, if the doctors had been right, the children and I would have been mourning instead of laughing.

As Don and I unpacked the ornaments we'd collected over the years, we told Jay and Holly the story behind each purchase. In one box was the lopsided, red plastic treetop spire we'd had since our first Christmas together. Even now that we could afford something nicer, we'd refused to replace a symbol of those early years of adjustment, instead laughing at the early minicrises we'd created for ourselves.

I'd flippantly told my sister cancer took the fun out of a good argument, but Don and I had finally learned the joy of treasuring *this* moment instead of hanging our happiness on the future. And in the midst of that growth, we'd learned to thank God for His daily miracles of normal activities instead of demanding that He heal in our way.

The holidays were over all too quickly, and it was time

for the alarm to go off at 5:00 A.M. again. Gradually our routines were getting back to normal. Normal. That ironic word again.

In early January, Don was scheduled for more chemotherapy. I took the day off and, armed with my needlepoint, began the long wait with my Scotsman. Randall, his usual companion, had taken a job at Tennessee's University of the South, so I knew Don would miss talking about football. I had quickly scanned the sports page, memorizing a few names. Maybe I couldn't "talk" football with my husband, but my questions would keep us occupied during the waiting.

At last a treatment chair was available. As Don waited for the nurse to start the IV, he suddenly gasped. I was at his side immediately. "Donnie, what's wrong?"

He shook his head. "I hate this. I hate this chemo."

I squeezed his shoulder but could say nothing. Where was his fighting Scots spirit? If he couldn't tolerate the intolerable, he'd lose. *Lord, please keep him strong.*

He went ahead with the treatment, but the following morning, his despondency lingered. He insisted I go to work, saying he wanted the house quiet so he could sleep.

"Do you want to talk first?" I asked.

He shrugged. "It's getting harder for me to take those treatments. Why don't I just give up? I gain heaven that way."

I tried to keep the panic out of my voice. "Of course this whole thing is terrible. But you've got to keep fighting. We need you. *I* need you. Remember?"

He only shrugged. All the way to school, I prayed, asking the Lord to give him special strength for the day. One of our friends had said he admired our philosophy that helped us pull out the positive aspects of each problem. If only he could see the battle we were in now.

My lesson plans for mythology class that day included a discussion of the Norsemen's valor. As much as I admired their ideals of "dying well" (bravely), they had to fight alone, seldom aided by divine intervention. Their only hope was in the battle itself. I identified with their struggles.

As soon as I arrived, I hurried to Carl Amann's room, anxious to tell my Christian "big brother" the latest trauma. His eyes filled with tears.

"Don's got to keep fighting," he said. "People are forgetting to pray now that the initial shock has worn off. Let them know you need those prayers."

I felt better after talking with Carl, but I still called Don to check on him. He sounded cheerful, saying he'd given himself a good scolding for scaring me. He just wouldn't think about the treatments until the next one.

Maybe he wouldn't, but I would. My prayers that day weren't very saintly. Don's side pain always increased after the chemotherapy, so I cried for help. We had believed, we had prayed, we had done what we could, yet the pain still persisted. *Don't you care, God?*

That night, I read numerous psalms, marveling at the verses reminding me we weren't alone. At last I went to bed, falling asleep to the sound of Don's peaceful breathing.

The cold winter days fell into manageable patterns. Don still loved teaching two hours each day, and I was juggling my duties. And both of us were sleeping better each night. Then just as our schedule settled, Holly fell at a friend's house.

While normal children's stumbles cause bad bruises, hers resulted in stitches, for the skin had split upon impact—just as Don's had at her age. By the time I arrived at the emergency room, Don was hovering over

Holly while two nurses held her legs. The shots had begun to take effect, and she was no longer screaming. From Don's expression, I knew the gash was bad. In fact, it took 37 stitches.

Outwardly I made motherly sounds of comfort, but I was seething. Why couldn't her skin be tougher? Why did she have to go to the emergency room when other kids just put ice on purple spots? Earlier she'd called this her "happy day" since she and Suzie Morris had so many fun things planned.

Now she was in the emergency room again. Mingling with thoughts of her ruined plans were those of the lost dreams her dad and I had carried. Well, both awful things had happened. We could do nothing now but try to get through them with God's help.

Then I thought of those children in the radiation department, wearing baseball caps on bald heads. Thirty-seven stitches was nothing. And Don was teaching instead of being bedridden. Everything could have been much worse. *Thank you, Father.*

* * *

Between editorial changes on Marta's book and the typical crises, we lost February. Suddenly it was March and time for another CAT scan and chemotherapy. Don's brother Doug drove down from Flint to be with us for the day. On the way out the door, I reminded Don to get his cane, but he shook his head.

"Nope. I'm going to give them a clear CAT scan today. I'm through with canes."

As I saw his familiar grin, I realized he had been *carrying* his cane more than *using* it lately.

Suddenly I was excited about the appointment.

After the scan, Don performed the usual antics for Dr. Silver to show brain activity: standing on one foot with his eyes closed, rapidly touching his finger to the doctor's hand, then to his own nose and back to the hand. After he did each flawlessly, Dr. Silver casually mentioned he was surprised. Then he called for the scan report.

"Well, remarkably, it's clear," Dr. Silver reported.

Quick looks of joy crossed our faces. "That means he's through with chemotherapy, right?" I asked Dr. Silver.

Apologetically, he shook his head. The treatments had to continue to rid the system of other cancer cells undoubtedly lurking within Don's system. Our joy dissolved.

In that moment, an invisible blanket of comfort gently dropped around my shoulders. When the time came for Don to get off of the chemotherapy, God would help him make that decision.

"But for how long?" I asked. "Why can't you tell us a specific number of treatments, the way they did in radiology?"

Dr. Silver answered carefully. "Unfortunately, we haven't had enough positive response to this cancer to make a judgment."

I turned to Don. "How do you feel?" I teased. "They haven't had anybody else live this long with a brain metastasis."

Dr. Silver was solemn. "Essentially that is the situation, Mrs. Aldrich. Medically, we will come to the time when you must make a decision. If we stop the chemo-therapy too early, the cancer can come back—stronger than before—and we may be unable to control it. And if we keep Mr. Aldrich on this massive treatment schedule too long, it may cause other types of cancer."

Suddenly I couldn't breathe! My ever-present outward calm had forced me to hear that. *Please, Father, help us.*

In that moment, an invisible blanket of comfort gently dropped around my shoulders. When the time came for Don to get off of the chemotherapy, God would help him make that decision. For now we would rejoice in the remission!

* * *

The next week, the father of one of our friends died. His lung cancer supposedly had been milder, and the doctors had told him he would live to be an old man. Instead he had heard only the word "cancer" and had given up.

My mind spun. Where does the direct touch of the Lord stop—or begin—and where does the individual's courage take over? Why had Don's severe cancer gone into remission, while this man's supposedly mild form proved fatal? What part did prayer have in all of this? Can that change God's mind?

The next night, Holly asked me to read a story to her. It was already well past her bedtime, so I agreed to only one. We curled up together in the red chair and enjoyed the adventures of a lost teddy bear. At the happy ending, I gave her a hug and eased her off my lap. Instead she asked for another story.

"No, Holly. I said only one."

"Oh, please, Mommy," she whispered. "I like sitting here with you. Just one more."

Of course I read another one. Now I had even more to ponder. Is that what God had done in our crisis? The previous summer I had known something bad was going to happen. I sensed finality, and knew I was being prepared for something awful. When it came on that August morning, the doctors said Don's death could occur within a matter of weeks, maybe even days, and that we couldn't hope for remission. And yet, he had astounded everyone.

The next morning when Barin Lenze, one of my coworkers, asked about Don, I tried to verbalize my questions. His wife had survived cancer too, so he understood.

"Maybe it's like standing in the middle of a big circle," he said. "If you have good peripheral vision, you see things around you even at the side. If you have tunnel vision, you see only what's directly in front of you. But either way, no one sees behind, and, thus, no one sees the whole circle all at once. So you just keep praying and walking by faith—and treasuring every extra moment you have together."

I carried those thoughts as we told our friends about Don's remission. Some insisted we had to stop the chemotherapy, saying we weren't showing faith that God could keep the cancer from coming back. Then the newspaper reported two cases of parents charged with manslaughter because their children died after medical treatment was withheld. Neither set of parents were part of any fanatical religious group; they just claimed God's healing and had refused medicines. I had long ago conceded my lack of answers. All we could do was give each day to the Lord and ask for His guidance.

* * *

The winter was hanging on, so for exercise we started

bowling. Jay and Holly had never bowled, so they giggled as ball after ball plopped into the gutter. Don told them about our first bowling date in college, laughing that he'd been upset because I'd beaten him. I confessed that in typical Southern-girl fashion, I'd tried to throw gutter balls, only to have them hook and turn into strikes.

Soon we were laughing about those early dates, especially the days of calling professors by nicknames, using cafeteria trays as sleds and kissing in the snowbank when we collided. Jay and Holly looked bored; those memories belonged only to the two of us and couldn't be translated.

Don bowled three strikes in a row in spite of his painful side. I marveled that he was the same man who'd leaned heavily on a cane just a few months before. But after one particularly energetic throw, I noticed him gently rub his side and hitch his shoulder. When he sat down, I patted his hand.

"Donnie, how do you tolerate that pain?" I asked.

He gave me one of those patient looks usually reserved for the times I had tried to balance the checkbook. "San, remember that day in the park when I asked the Lord to help me with it? Well, there's nothing to do *but* tolerate it."

* * *

Gradually the winter gave way to swollen tree buds and deep blue skies. I loved pointing out a clump of daffodils and turning to Don for his grin of appreciation.

In addition to daffodils, April brought the tennis season I'd been dreading. Even with remission, I thought the shingles pain would keep him off the coaching staff. But the athletic director was happy to have him back. Don grinned at the news. "See? I told you last summer that with God's help I'd be back on the courts! This year the high school, next year Wimbledon!"

Just before the season opened, two important things happened: I gave Don a surprise thirty-ninth birthday party, and the four of us drove to Nashville to see Randall and his family. In the past, driving 800 miles in a day was nothing to him, but the side pain forced us to take two days. Some things not even a positive attitude could conquer.

His birthday, the trip and coaching would have made a marvelous month if my beloved Uncle Lawrence Farley hadn't suffered a massive heart attack and died. Even though I'd known how desperately ill he was, I still was unprepared when he died. How could someone who had always been in my life be dead?

Adding to my anguish was my inability to attend his funeral in Kentucky. The trip would be too hard for Don so soon after Nashville, and he refused to let me go without him. He said he'd worry. Oh, it was OK if I worried about him *all* the time, but he didn't want to worry about me for two days?

He sighed with patient exasperation. "Look, San, I know you can get along without me, but I can't get along without you. And I need you *here*, where I don't have to worry about you."

Those words calmed me for a while, but soon I complained about *his* relatives not even acknowledging his illness while Uncle Lawrence had written and called numerous times. Don started to answer me in kind, but suddenly stopped. "Hey, San, you're bummed because you can't be there. And you have every right to be!"

Bummed! What a refreshingly honest word. I knelt next to his chair and cried with my head against his lap. As he stroked my hair, he talked about the heavenly home-coming Uncle Lawrence must have had. I nodded, thinking of my grandparents as young marrieds, waiting for their children to arrive one by one. Now they were in heaven, again waiting.

Don turned my face to his. "Just think. While your cousin Joyce was patting his arm *here,* he was hugging Papa and Mama *there.*"

During the following weeks, Don's coaching, school activities and parenting kept us busy. I hadn't felt well, but blamed it on a late night of checking final drafts of Marta's book. Then I developed a fever. When I finally went to our family doctor, he discovered an enlarged liver. He insisted on bed rest as well as medication, but I argued I had a family to run. It was only his threat of a potentially serious problem that caused me to give in. Still the fever persisted.

Don was concerned I was sick because of having to care for him, but I didn't worry about a cause. I just wanted to be well.

One afternoon, when Mother called, I told her about the tests scheduled to determine the cause of the enlarged liver. Quietly she offered her own solution.

"Honey, I think you've just got a bad case of the 'can't help its' because of losing your Uncle Lawrence."

"Don't get me started, Mother!"

"I'm not trying to. But you just think about that when you're praying."

When we hung up, I shook my head over her simple solution. Stress caused headaches, not enlarged livers and undiagnosed fevers. But as I thought of Uncle Lawrence again, I started to sob. I remembered the bouquet of dog-wood blossoms he'd given me during my senior year, the trips to the rock quarry deep into Pine Mountain, his promise to tell me the truth about the family shooting in the 1930s and . . . .

"Look, God," I finally prayed, "I'm angry at you for letting him die. I know that's a sin, but I'm not ready to ask forgiveness. I am willing to talk about it though."

So I began—with eyes wide open and tears flowing—to talk. I complained not only about his death, but the circumstances that kept me from going to his funeral—Don's cancer, the chemotherapy, his side pain. A human would have told me to pull myself together with the old life-goes-on remark. But as I prayed, I felt surrounded by compassion. Only when my anger was spent, did I allow Him to comfort me.

The next day I went back to our doctor for another exam. Of course, the fever was down and the liver was normal. At his astonishment over the recovery, I told him about my anger, adding a sorrowful, "Why didn't you ask me what was going on in my life?"

He shook his head. "I didn't think I had to ask *you* that."

I had just learned a valuable lesson—one I would need someday.

CHAPTER FOUR

Prayer at Midnight

June 25, 1982
Muskegon, Michigan

Shortly after school was out in June, we left for Maranatha. What a thrill it was to be back—especially after the frightening events of the previous summer. I tried not to think about Don's having asked for "just one more summer at Maranatha." He was in remission; I wouldn't harbor negative thoughts.

The summer was beautiful. Each day we did what we wanted: Don enjoyed tennis and golf, Jay and Holly played with their friends, and I made curtains and cooked. So why was I waiting for the other shoe to drop?

One of the golfers, Bob Jelsema, was a builder who decided to replace our old deck. Arguing with a Dutchman is useless, especially one who wants to use his skills to express love.

Morrie and Denny helped too. Don's talents didn't

include construction, but he'd hammer the rusted nails out of still-usable boards. One afternoon he worked long after the others had left. As I handed him a glass of ice water, I noticed he had hitched his left shoulder. The side pain was bad.

"Don, why don't you quit? You've done enough for today."

He took a deep drink and handed the glass back. "No. I like doing this," he said. "For once I can see results. Every year, I wonder if I've made a difference in any student's life. At least this lets me see where I've started and where I'm going to end. I was just thinking that if I had to do it over again, I'd be a carpenter."

I thought of the work he'd put into his master's and specialist's degrees, and sat down on the closest step.

"Don, do you want to move?" I asked. "Remission gave you a second chance at life; let's do something with it. Remember when you were little and wanted to be a truck driver? I'll teach while you train for a new career. And I'll do it with minimum complaining."

He chuckled at my last comment, but shook his head. "No, I don't want to do anything other than what I'm doing. I guess I just wanted to know I've made a difference, that's all."

* * *

The only bad part of the summer was the continued chemotherapy. Every four weeks, we left Jay and Holly with my parents and then drove to the hospital. One afternoon, a new doctor thrust his hand toward Don.

"I want to meet the 'miracle man'! I've been following your case with interest."

Don beamed. "Well, the credit goes to the Lord."

Most doctors gave us a polite smile when we made comments like that. But this one leaned against the window sill. "I'll accept your explanation because I don't have a better one," he said. "Radiation didn't do this. Nor chemotherapy. As much as I want our department to be able to take the credit for this cancer to seemingly disappear, we can't."

I ignored the word "seemingly" and pounced upon the rest of the sentence. "Then why does he have to continue these awful treatments?" I asked.

He nodded. "Because we don't know they're useless either. If the chemotherapy *is* doing what it's supposed to, it would be dangerous to stop at this point. But we will spread out the treatments over the next six months. Fair enough?"

As much as we didn't like it, we agreed. My major frustration that day was the disinterest an examining intern showed as I told her about the drastic changes we'd made in our diet. Her casual, "We don't know the value of such alterations" astounded me. What about rickets and scurvy? Both were major problems until their nutritional elements were discovered. Diet *has* to be a major key in cancer's cure.

But Don had leaned forward when the intern dismissed the importance of what we were doing; he hated choking down massive vitamins each morning. Something in his eyes told me he'd just freed himself from that ritual.

* * *

Our weeks at Maranatha were passing all too quickly. In late August, we packed a light picnic and walked to a favorite spot far down the beach. The waves were perfect for body surfing, so we swam before supper. Don and I tired long before Jay and Holly did, so we sat on the sand, watching them and listening to "Dad! Watch this!" or "Hey, Mom! Look!"

We called encouragements, but gradually Don merely smiled to acknowledge their accomplishments. I asked if his side was especially painful, but he shook his head.

"No, San, I was just thinking how much I'm enjoying being here. This is all I want—to be able to spend time with my family. I wish I could call back the times I chose to be away."

As he put his arm around me in that old protecting way, I leaned against his chest, wanting to hold that moment forever.

* * *

On the last Saturday in August, Don's golfing buddies had their annual luncheon. Last year, they had been somber. This year the lane in front of Morrie and Gert's place was filled with banter as each golfer arrived.

Don kept on his yellow golf hat, still self-conscious about the fuzz covering his head, but his eyes sparkled as the gag gifts were awarded. First place was a red garage-sale coat—the color of champions. Denny, who had missed a birdie, was awarded a butcher's chicken dressed in a golfer's suit. A collective howl went up, filling me with joy.

The official awards of "Best Golfer" and "Most Improved" were given with teasing too. After each wisecrack, the men grinned at Don, happy to be sharing the joke with him.

After the trophies for excellence had been given, one more came out of the box. "And this one goes to the Maranatha Player of the Year, whose attitude and spirit were an inspiration to us all—Don Aldrich!"

As the men whistled and clapped, Don beamed. Maybe he'd never know whether he'd made a difference in the students' lives, but he knew he'd touched the lives of his dear Maranatha buddies.

* * *

We closed our place just before Labor Day, anxious to get back to a normal life again. Then in the midst of making plans to teach full time, Don refused to continue chemotherapy.

The treatments had been getting rougher for both of us. My stomach churned as I anticipated the ordeal he faced every four weeks. Don dreaded even the preparations since it was difficult for the nurses to hit a good vein on the first try. Sometimes the drugs spilled into the surrounding tissues and his hand had to be packed in ice to keep down the swelling. Then we would have to watch for the beginnings of ulceration.

So when the September CAT scan showed no signs of the cancer, Don insisted upon release from the program. The decision frightened me, but I was relieved too. The freedom gave us a beautiful autumn. We went on family walks, even back to the park to collect the hickory nuts. Don jogged as I peeled the thick hull off each nut, remembering the pain as we sat there last year, trying not to listen to the soccer game.

* * *

Last year, our neighbors had taken turns mowing our yard. This year, Don could do that again. One afternoon I came around the house with the rose trimmers in my hand

and found him standing by the lawn mower, his eyes closed and his face toward the sun.

"Donnie?"

He turned. "Was it this beautiful last year?"

I nodded, remembering those prison days of watching others bound into their cars. Don gestured toward the trimmers.

"Do the roses later," he said. "It's time you learned how to run this so I can go golfing."

"No way," I retorted. "When Jay gets older, show him."

"What would you be doing if I had died last year?" Don asked. "Would Bill and Keith still be doing the work?"

Another argument lost. Within a few minutes the self-propelled mower was jerking me—an overweight German—around the yard. Apparently I looked just as ridiculous as I felt because Don was holding his painful side and roaring his unique laugh. Jay and Holly came to the front yard to see what was going on, and Keith and Betty looked up from their own yard work. Everyone thought it was enormously funny. I stopped the mower.

"That's my entertainment for today; I'll get back to my roses now."

"Ah, San, don't be angry," Don said. "But you ought to know how to do things like this." Suddenly the memory of my being jerked around like some giant rag doll was too much for him and he folded into laughter again.

* * *

Now that Don's health had improved, we had time to concentrate upon other crises—such as our brothers' and sisters' family problems or our parents' health. We were especially troubled about my mother since she had occasional chest pains but refused to see a doctor. Don threatened to hog-tie her and take her himself, but she'd just murmured, "Honey, would you really do that to your poor ole mother-in-law?"

He flashed his familiar grin. "Sure would. I need you around to keep praying. Besides, nobody makes butterscotch pies the way you do. So you better promise you'll go the next time those pains start."

Of course she promised, but for some strange reason they didn't occur again. That was a relief since I was already struggling with my new assignment at the junior high, Jay and Holly's progress in school and Don's constant side pain. If it hadn't been for his going to bed so early, we would have considered ourselves a normal family. I was even beginning to sleep through the night for the first time in months.

When Don's side pain had increased the previous year, he had apologetically asked me to move out of our double bed. He'd teasingly offered me visitation rights, but neither of us was happy with the decision. Still, I rearranged the furniture and added a single bed. Even from across the room, my internal alarm still had sounded whenever Don sat up during the night. Sometimes he needed a pain pill, sometimes he was just trying to position the pillow against his tender side.

That autumn those frequent awakenings were finally a bad memory, as I discovered one morning when Don teased me.

"You were breathing so heavily I thought you were having a bad dream, San. I called to you several times before you stopped."

I was horrified. "That's terrible! What if you had needed me?"

He just chuckled. "Ah, come on. If I'd needed you, you

would have awakened. I just figured you were trying to pay me back for all those years I snored in your ear."

I worried we were becoming too normal.

I had reason to worry. Recently, we'd slipped into our old habits. When I told Don that for Marta's publisher I'd listed archaeology as one of my interests, he gave me an oh-sure look.

"What does that mean?" I snapped.

He shrugged. "That's the first I've heard about any interest in archaeology. Who you trying to impress?"

I didn't listen to those little alarms going off in my head; I exploded. The first he'd heard about it? Just what did he think classical mythology was based on? Why did he think I was willing to stand in long lines to see the artifacts from Pompeii and ancient Egypt?

I glared at him. We were back to normal all right.

He didn't shrug. "Ah, San, I tell everyone else how much you mean to me, but I don't tell you. Let's be friends, huh?"

His usual plea was said in a little-boy voice that always cracked my defense. Admitting defeat, I leaned against his chest as his arms went around me.

"Hey, yesterday we filled out information sheets for the school yearbook," he said. "One of the questions asked which person we most admire. Guess who I listed?"

Boy, he had an amazing ability to forget an argument quickly. OK, I'd play my part.

"I'd guess that big tennis star what's-his-name, if it was based just on ability," I said. "But I know you don't like his attitude. It has to be a sports figure though. Give me a hint."

He pulled back to look at me. "Ah, San, it's *you.*"

Me? But I'd gained weight and had changed from the timid 20-year-old he'd married. I stared at him, struggling with my years of low self-esteem, but found no hint of the clown's teasing in his deep blue eyes. I leaned against his chest again, marveling at the delicious sound of "the one I most admire."

* * *

On the afternoon of Jay's tenth birthday in early October, Don came home with a second-place trophy for the school's annual tennis tournament. I squealed, but he shook his head.

"I should have won first place. I must have pulled a muscle that slowed me down."

My mind refused to register the comment about the muscle. "Don! This time last year, the doctors were waiting for you to die. You're complaining because you took *second* place in a tournament this year!"

He grinned. "Hey, when you're used to being number one, it's hard to settle for second. What's for dinner?"

He didn't mention the pulled muscle again. A few weeks later, we attended the Maranatha Board of Directors meeting in Grand Rapids. The trauma of last year was lost as I watched him play with Jay and Holly in the motel pool. I sat in a deck chair, working on the Pharaoh and whispering prayers of thanksgiving.

That weekend we even had a re-run of the special breakfast Phyllis DeVries had prepared the year before. As we lingered over coffee, Don excused himself, hoping to ease his side in a soft living room chair.

Gradually the discussion at the table turned to whatever-happened-to questions as they talked about a mutual friend who had died several years ago. As I sipped my coffee, I sensed it would someday be like this for Don too.

People would remember him, smile at his name and talk about him over coffee.

Suddenly I was lonesome for him and left the table to sit beside him. His gentle smile welcomed me.

We never mentioned the breakfast remembrances during the long ride home; Don wanted details of my Thanksgiving menu. That holiday meal had always been his favorite, so I spared no effort. We always had a 22-pound turkey with the traditional dishes and invited as many relatives as we could crowd into our home.

The holiday day was just as perfect as we had planned. Even though he'd mentioned that his legs hurt from all of his sports activities, we'd ignored the warning. After all, he'd just been to our family doctor, who'd taken Xrays. When nothing showed up, he gave Don muscle-relaxant tablets, saying his legs had been overcompensating for the pain in his side and, thus, put more strain on his legs.

Now with Don sitting in front of a perfectly cooked turkey, I couldn't believe anything could be wrong. His blond hair was growing back and his beard was as full as ever. In his beige sweater, he looked especially handsome as his banter kept the laughter crossing from table to table. Several relatives commented on how well he looked, adding they hadn't thought he'd live to see another Thanksgiving. I tried not to hear that.

The following week, Don went back to his sports, but something was wrong. One evening, he mentioned he'd fallen while returning a low shot in racquetball. My head jerked up, but he was concentrating on buttering his whole wheat muffin. Neither of us wanted to face what we knew was ahead.

Praying about the pain became a regular part of our family devotions. Hot baths relaxed the tight muscles, so we wanted to believe our local doctor. Don was scheduled for a January appointment at University of Michigan; this could wait until then.

* * *

But even as I outwardly went through our busy days, the great what-ifs were back. What if the cancer were out of remission? What if he died?

While I struggled with new battles, John Sherrill, my editor, called with a status report on Marta's book and to check on Don. As I told him about the leg pain, I poured out my frustration.

But even as I outwardly went through our busy days, the great what-ifs were back. What if the cancer were out of remission? What if he died?

"About the time I think I'm being victorious, fear comes sweeping in," I said. "Then the battle begins all over again. I want so much for my Christian walk to be just that. But it's always a battle."

John chuckled. "Who told you it was supposed to be a walk? It's a slugfest. Don's fortunate to have you as a warrior by his side. While he's battling the pain, you're battling on a different level."

I'd never thought of myself as a *spiritual* warrior, but I hugged his encouragement to me.

* * *

I had started taking the Pharaoh needlepoint to school so I could work on it for a few minutes during lunch and finish in time for Christmas. Each noon, I'd prop my Bible open on my desk, position the needle, and read the next verse as I pulled the thread through. But on the Monday after John called, I often lost my place thinking about something Don had said the night before. He'd watched Holly tenderly tuck a blanket around her doll and said, "You know she gets that mothering from you."

"Me?!"

He nodded. "She really identifies with you."

Suddenly we were talking about people's different reactions to grief as we tried to define the thin line between honest pain and interpreting sorrow as a personal zap from God.

Come to think of it, Jay and Holly hadn't been arguing over who would sit next to their dad at the restaurants anymore. Instead, Holly had been content to slide in next to me. I bit my lip. The family structure had been changing as steadily as Don's returning hair, and I'd been too busy to notice.

Don had continued. "You're stronger than you think, San. If it hadn't been for you, I would have died last year."

I shuddered. "Oh, Don, if you had died, would that have been my fault?"

He'd laughed. "I hadn't thought of it that way." Suddenly we were talking about people's different reactions to grief as we tried to define the thin line between honest pain and interpreting sorrow as a personal zap from God.

"Don't be like that, San," was all Don had said.

Now in my empty classroom, as I forced myself to concentrate on Ephesians, I realized verse after verse was warning me of battle. Don's cancer *was* back! I dropped the needlepoint and sobbed.

School couldn't get out fast enough that day. I had to get Don back to his U of M doctor. Why had we been so blind? Why wouldn't we face what we knew?

When I arrived at Don's school, I greeted him with "we have to go to the hospital."

He nodded. "I know. Today my feet are wooden, just like last fall. I'll call my doctor as soon as we get home."

While he described the pain to the specialist, I made arrangements for Jay and Holly to stay next door with the Thompsons. Then just before we left, the four of us stood by our front door and joined hands. Don was the sick one; I should have been the one to pray. But I shook my head sorrowfully as I looked at him. If I spoke, I'd lose what little stamina I had.

I marveled that Don's voice didn't crack. "Well, here we go again, Lord. Please be with us. Protect Jay and Holly, and keep San strong. And please give me courage."

I drove to the hospital while Don rubbed his legs. His cane, once discarded, now rested against his knee.

"San, all day I've thought what if I have to be in a wheelchair the rest of my life. Maybe we'll have to buy a van with one of those special lifts."

I offered quick encouragement. "Now aren't you glad you didn't marry a Size Three? I'll lug you all over the United States, if you want."

He grinned as he patted my abundant thigh. "Yep. You always said I had to have the biggest and best."

* * *

I waited impatiently in a folding chair for Don to be brought back from more tests. Why wouldn't they let me be with him in the scan room? Surely they could have eased the rules since it was almost 10 o'clock. We needed to be together.

Shortly, the examining doctor approached, saying I should go to the room he'd ordered on Nine North. I stared at him. Nine North? But that was for terminal patients. He stammered something about it being the best room available and turned away. I gathered our coats, Don's hat and cane, and walked through the dark, twisting hallways.

A nurse on Nine North escorted me to a room and suggested I sleep while I waited for the remaining test. But I couldn't; I wanted to be with Don mentally. *Please Lord, help him not to have a reaction to the dyes. Please let him feel your presence.*

Just before midnight, the examining doctor entered the room. How tired he looked. I gestured to the chair next to mine. He looked far too young to handle life-and-death situations. He ought to be escorting some 17-year-old to the junior banquet.

"Mr. Aldrich will be returning from the tests soon."

"The cancer's back, isn't it?"

He looked startled. "Mrs. Aldrich, your husband asked me not to say anything to you other than to let you know he's out of testing. We'll talk in the morning."

"I know the cancer's back. I just don't know how bad it is," I snapped. "If you were one of his regular doctors, you'd know I don't like games like this. I have to know exactly what I'm dealing with so I can know how to fight it."

The young man wanted to be anyplace but in that room. "Mrs. Aldrich, your husband has asked that he be the one to tell you."

I nodded, too tired to talk anymore.

A few minutes later Don was brought in. I sat on the bed, my face over his. He took a deep breath, then put his hand to my cheek.

"Well, San, we've got our work cut out for us. The cancer's back, and the lesions are bigger than ever."

I leaned my head against his chest and whispered, "Oh, Donnie. You're my whole life."

He stroked my hair. "I know," was all he could say.

* * *

The next morning, Dr. Neubig—a bearded young man whose shoulder twitched as he gave us the serious results of each test—reported that the cancer was also in the spinal fluid. They'd put Don back on standard chemotherapy since it apparently had worked before. But this time, they'd give him an amnesiac, so he wouldn't remember the treatment's harshness. They were hoping the treatments would take care of both the brain lesions and the spinal fluid cancer. Me too; I kept remembering Don's comment about being in a wheelchair.

During the treatment, I sat on one side of the bed and the nurse on the other. Don put his unrestricted arm around me and pulled me close to him. "Just remember, San," he said. "The Lord never promised to give us an easy road, but He did promise to always be with us."

With my tears dropping onto his face, I whispered our prayer for healing and for strength. How warm and sweet Don's breath was on my lips as he whispered "Amen" with me.

Once the drug took effect, Don slept deeply. Occasionally he'd suddenly sit up and look around. I'd murmur, "I'm here" and he'd lie back down.

As I waited, I worked on the needlepoint or read the

Bible. Perhaps we were merely in Round Two. With the Lord's help, we were prepared to go the full 15 rounds if that's what He wanted. I turned to Ephesians 6:11, rereading the instructions to put on *God's* armor, rather than our own feeble weapons.

Don was released late that afternoon. Dr. Neubig gave me a list of symptoms to watch for and stressed that Don wasn't to return to work until further notice. The amnesiac had worked: My stubborn Scotsman was insisting he felt fine, convinced this had been his mildest chemotherapy. When I assured Dr. Neubig he'd rest until next's week's appointment, we were allowed to go.

At home, I helped Don to bed, gently pulling the quilts over his shoulders. After putting Jay and Holly to bed, I eased between my own sheets and fell into exhausted sleep.

In the middle of the night, I suddenly awakened. Just as I started to get up to check on Don, I heard him whisper, "Thank you, Lord." Then he prayed for all of us, still in a whisper. He asked for strength for me and for courage for himself. Then after a moment's pause, he whispered again.

"And Lord, please use this to cause family members to think about you. Let them see your reality. . . and please let that happen while I can still see it, Lord, if it's your will. And help me to be especially kind to San and not get upset when she tells me I can't do something. I know she's right. She's suffered so much. Please give her a special blessing out of this. And thank you again for letting me be home."

At his whispered, "amen," I spoke. "Donnie? Can I get you anything?"

"No, I'm OK. You were listening, weren't you? And to think I had to yell at you this summer to get your attention."

How good it was to hear that quiet chuckle in the darkness. He'd been right this summer too: When I thought he needed me, I had awakened immediately. I no longer worried I would sleep through a crisis.

CHAPTER FIVE

Donnie, You're Free!

December 17, 1982
Canton, Michigan

The morning after Don's midnight prayer, he insisted I return to my classroom, saying he was fine. He seemed cheerful, but I was especially troubled that day about leaving him alone.

As I dropped Jay and Holly at their school, I asked, "Why is this day so different, Lord?"

I didn't like the answer that settled into my spirit: "Yea, though he slay me yet will I trust him."

I gasped. "Lord, if you take Don you might as well take me too. He's my whole life. How will I survive without my clown?"

All the way to school, I cried, begging God not to take Don. I even reminded Him of His own Son's prayer, "If it be Thy will let this cup pass from me."

But also like His Son, I had to complete that prayer with "not my will but Thine." Then, with tears running down my cheeks, I dared to ask two things.

"But please don't let Don be alone when that happens. And please give us Christmas."

I don't remember driving to school that morning, but suddenly I was in the staff parking lot. I hurried to my room and opened my Bible to the verse I'd heard within my heart, Job 13:15: "Though he slay me, yet will I trust him." I pushed my flushed face to the cool pages, knowing that whatever was about to happen was from God's hand. But even that assurance didn't diminish its horror.

Students began to fill the halls then, so I busied myself by putting the vocabulary list on the board. That was the longest day I'd ever taught. I even called Don twice, holding my breath until he picked up the receiver.

Surely I drove home that day, but all I remember is rushing through the front door and seeing Don sitting in his orange chair, smiling. Oh, what a beautiful sight!

His third hour class had sent candy and a huge card filled with get well wishes and promises of prayer. Don's eyes sparkled. "Maybe I've touched a few lives after all."

While he was still reading the messages, a poinsettia was delivered from the girl's tennis team and their coaches. I set it on the hearth, where he could see it best.

Now that Christmas vacation had begun and I could be home with him every day, I watched his every move, trying to analyze deterioration. But whenever I asked about his feet, he insisted they didn't feel any different. He was determined to make it to Christmas. He knew if he went back into the hospital, he'd have to spend the holiday there.

Finally on that Wednesday before Christmas, I called our pastor, Dr. Bartlett Hess, and asked for the elders to anoint Don with oil, as prescribed in the book of James. Even as a good Presbyterian, I didn't want to leave one stone unturned.

But this anointing brought no peace for me.

After Dr. Hess and the others left, I helped Don upstairs to bed. His breathing was labored. I wondered what part of me was ruled by cautious concern and what by absolute fear. Please Lord, you be in charge—not my fears.

As I pulled off his slippers, Don said he couldn't feel his feet. Both were so cold that even my rubbing them didn't restore feeling. I called his doctor, knowing we'd have to report to the hospital immediately. Our neighbor Bill Fife would stay with the sleeping Jay and Holly.

Because of the shortened staff over the holidays, Don was assigned to a 20-bed ward. Then another round of tests and questions began. By 2 A.M. the decision to do an immediate lumbar puncture was made. They would draw out spinal fluid and replace it with the same amount of chemotherapy. The doctor pulled back the curtain.

"Mrs. Aldrich, please wait outside," he said.

I looked directly at him. "No. I'm going to sit in this corner and work on my needlepoint. And when you see my head down, ignore me. I won't be passed out; I'll be praying."

He moved toward the bed without another word.

For 30 minutes I prayed silently as they made repeated attempts to find that spot between the vertebrate where the needle had to go. But Don's side pain wasn't allowing him to pull his body into the proper curl position. With each of his low moans, my stomach tightened that much more. Finally I stood up and faced the doctors.

"OK, I've had it. Now you *better* let me help. I'm through listening to you hurt him."

The resident glanced at the intern. Was he thinking of hospital regulations? Finally he spoke. "All right. Maybe if you pulled him into a tight curl. His spine has just enough curvature to make it difficult to insert the needle properly."

I leaned down and kissed Don's perspiration-soaked cheek.

"Come on, Donnie. We'll do it this time."

My right arm went around his shoulders, my left one under his knees. Bracing my legs against the bed, I pulled with all my Kentucky might.

"That's it! Now hold him just like that" the doctor said.

For an eternity neither of us moved. Every fiber in my shoulders screamed for release. *If only I could move just a little . . . no, just a few more minutes.*

With my mouth close to Don's ear I whispered prayers. "Thank you, Lord, for being with us. Thank you for the goodness you will bring out of this."

Somehow the minutes passed and he was allowed to uncurl. Both doctors nodded their thanks to me. Apparently they passed the word along too; in future lumbar punctures, even the new interns waited for me to take my position before beginning the procedure.

* * *

I went home to sleep for two hours and then was back at the hospital by 7:30. Just as I turned the corner to Don's ward, he was coming out of his cubicle—seated in a wheelchair! The very thing we had dreaded was now a reality. But none of that mattered as I saw the big grin on my Scotsman's face.

"Oh, San! I'm glad you're here," he said. "You can help me bathe."

I leaned over to kiss him. "OK, but I get to drive."

As I pushed the wheelchair, Don turned to look up at

me. "You know, this isn't going to be so bad after all."

Looking down at him, I turned the corner too sharply. The wheel caught, slamming the chair into the wall.

I gasped, but Don chuckled. "Maybe I better rephrase that."

In the middle of the hospital hall, I threw my arms around his shoulders and kissed the top of his head. Together we laughed with the joy of being together.

Wheelchairs didn't matter anymore. And neither did upholding the image of the Perfect Family opening the Perfect Gifts while sitting in front of the Perfect Tree. Just being together was Christmas enough. Even Jay and Holly understood that. They'd suggested we wait to open presents until their dad could be home with them.

Wheelchairs didn't matter anymore. And neither did upholding the image of the Perfect Family opening the Perfect Gifts while sitting in front of the Perfect Tree. Just being together was Christmas enough.

Since Don was scheduled to spend Christmas in the hospital, his brothers Dale and Doug planned to join us there for our annual Christmas Eve gathering. But the next morning a very excited Don called to report that the doctors had been so pleased by his progress they'd given him a three-day pass.

"Hurry and get me out of here!" was his joyful demand. A quick call to Flint to relay the news and I was out the door.

All of Don's medicines came home too, along with the strict time schedule. It meant having to set the alarm for several times during the night, but that was a small matter. We were going to be together for Christmas—at home.

As the prescriptions were given to us, the doctor warned about not mixing them with alcohol. But since we didn't have even wine in the house, we barely heard the warning.

One of the drugs would take a while to prepare, so I took Don home to be with his brothers and then drove the 30 miles back to the hospital pharmacy.

When I arrived home the second time, Don was drinking a glass of wine! Aghast, I grabbed the goblet from his hand. Heavy silence descended, so Don tried, in his usual peacemaking way, to soothe over another crisis.

"Ah, come on, San. That was only my second glass. It isn't as though I drank the whole bottle."

Second glass! I wanted to yell at Dale and Doug for giving him the wine. Instead I looked at Don, meaning to snap "Baloney!" Unfortunately, a similar-sounding swear word was my awful retort. As soon as the word was out of my mouth, I stopped, absolutely stunned. Don took one look at my horrified face and started to laugh. Dale jumped up from the chair, threw his arms around me, and shouted, "She's human after all!"

To cover the awkward moment, Doug reported the latest antics of one of their cousins. Soon they were remembering 1950s Christmas mornings when they had awakened each another for that trip down the stairs to the tree. As memory after memory rolled out, Don lapsed into silence. When the rest laughed at the image of a sleepy little Doug bumping into a long-ago door, Don remained somber.

"I guess I was mean that time, huh?" he said.

As they teased him, I thought *Tell him* now *that he was*

a good brother. Tell him now *that you love him.* But I said nothing; I'd already said too much.

The afternoon passed quickly. After they left, I cleaned the kitchen and asked Don if I could get him anything.

"No, just come and sit with me," he said.

He smiled as I positioned the cushion by his tender side and then sat across from him. "San, you're a saint," he said.

Suddenly tears were running down my cheeks. "No, I'm not! Saints don't yell obscene words as I did this afternoon."

He grinned. "Well, then you're my Saint Obscene. Ah, come on, don't be so hard on yourself. You're always saying the Lord brings good out of everything given to Him—let Him bring good out of even this."

Then his eyes sparkled with that familiar glow. "Saint Obscene. Actually, I think it has a nice ring to it."

* * *

That night Don read the Christmas story in Luke 2 and then read chapter after chapter as Jay and Holly leaned against his good side. If anyone had looked through the window, he would have seen the Perfect Family, reading the Perfect Story, in front of the Perfect Tree. But that was merely an image. We wanted nothing more than to remain together.

The next morning we were up before sunrise opening presents. As usual, Don and I delighted in watching the children open their packages before we exchanged our own gifts. When he unwrapped the ID bracelet I'd purchased as a last-minute gift, he beamed. "San! I've always wanted one of these! Thanks."

As he turned to adjust the chain, I sighed. Married almost 17 years and I'd never known he'd wanted an ID bracelet? What treasury of his thoughts and dreams were we about to lose? But I shook off the depressing thoughts. The doctors would have a new method waiting for us in a couple of days. We'd lick this problem yet—and be better people because of the experience. If I was going to think lack, I'd have lack. My jaw tightened with the determination to think only good thoughts.

Shortly, my family arrived. Then friends stopped by while the phone rang constantly. What a wonderfully zany day it was. And Don loved every minute. The heavy medication surely was morphine; for the first time in 16 months, he was free of pain.

Our three days together went all too quickly, but it gave me enough time to see changes in Don's personality. He had always been boisterous but now he was withdrawn, and the least noise made him jump. Then uncharacteristically, he snapped at Jay over something trivial. We could only stare at Don as we heard anger in his voice. Suddenly he looked frightened.

"San! What's wrong with me?!" he whispered.

I made some excuse about his being tired, but neither of us believed it. Something terrible was happening deep within him.

Two days after Christmas, it was time to return to the hospital. Before we left Jay and Holly with family, Don held them next to him for several moments.

* * *

On Don's ward, a doctor smiled at our cheerful report of the holiday. "Well, I'm glad we were able to get enough feeling into your feet to send you home."

Don refused to let him take credit. "No, I asked the Lord for Christmas, and *He* gave it."

I was only faintly aware of the doctor's polite reply as I turned to look at my Scotsman. He knew.

For the rest of the day, specialists arrived, shining lights into Don's eyes, trying to decide what to do next. His breathing was becoming labored whenever he sat up. And I'd noticed his chest was discolored after even a few steps. I mentioned that to one of the medical groups who came through. Only the red-haired doctor commented. His condescending manner irritated me.

"Tell me, Mrs. Aldrich, was the color reddish or bluish?"

Quickly I clutched my hands behind my back, wanting very much to smack him. I glared at him instead.

"It was a reddish blue. Look, this isn't his normal color. And this isn't his normal rate of breathing. He's never out of breath like this. I want this problem checked—now."

With a shrug, the doctor ordered chest Xrays, adding absent-mindedly that perhaps the cancer had spread to his lungs. When the results came back negative, the doctor gave a little smirk and said I was just overreacting. No, something was wrong, but I didn't have the medical knowledge to back my suspicions.

That afternoon, more specialists asked more questions as they wondered what to do with the one who had beaten their medical odds. Finally they decided to implant a reservoir in Don's scalp to eliminate the painful lumbar punctures. His surgery was scheduled for 7 A.M. the next day.

* * *

I awakened early, even before the alarm sounded, strangely troubled. My sister Greta was staying with Jay and Holly, so I hurriedly dressed. By six, Donnie and I were praying together.

When he was out of surgery and back into his ward, I sat close to his bed as he slept, watching his breath come from between his lips in sharp little puffs.

Dr. Neubig, our favorite Nine North doctor—and the one with the shoulder twitch—stopped in to check on Don. With him was Dr. Martin, an even younger-looking doctor in charge of the ward.

They gently awakened him, then reported they had ordered a lung scan in order to find the location of the blood clots undoubtedly causing the shortness of breath. Blood clots? Of course. That explained the discoloring. Why hadn't that red-haired doctor taken the time to listen to what I was trying to describe? I shook the anger off, trying to concentrate on what Dr. Martin was saying. The scans were ordered for noon, and Don wasn't to eat lunch. Don grumbled at that since he hadn't had breakfast because of the surgery. But Dr. Martin was insistent; the clots could be life-threatening.

When the porter came to take Don to the scan room, I asked if I could please accompany him. None of the others had allowed me in the test area, but she shrugged. "Sure. Come on."

As I helped Don sit up, he gestured toward the needle-point bag. "Might as well bring that too. These tests take forever."

In the scan room, he asked to see the Pharaoh again and then smiled sadly as I turned it toward him. Oh, I wish I'd been able to finish it long ago. Then the technician asked him to blow into a white tube so she could test his lung capacity. As I watched, I found myself puffing too, willing him my lung strength.

Then she asked him to lie on his stomach, holding his

breath, while the scan recorded the lung profile. I watched the familiar dots outline one full lung and then begin the top of the other. But the dots stopped. Nothing showed below the top quarter of the lung! I stared at the screen. *Oh, Father, it's going to be very soon, isn't it?*

Finally the tests were complete. I stood aside as orderlies put him on the gurney. Suddenly his face went white.

"Oh, I'm so dizzy," he said.

Oh, Father, help was the only prayer my pounding heart formed. Immediately, I felt tangible arms around me, squeezing my shoulders. I knew no one was near me.

Then he made one horrible, strangling sound, as his body arched. A technician ran for the doctor in the next room while I stood there, useless.

I couldn't watch as the doctor rushed in. All I could do was listen to those awful sounds.

Oh, Father, help was the only prayer my pounding heart formed. Immediately, I felt tangible arms around me, squeezing my shoulders. I knew no one was near me.

Suddenly Dr. Neubig ran in, helping turn Don on his side. Someone tried to get me to leave, but I shook my head.

"Leave her alone!" he commanded. "Get a code blue out. Now!" Dr. Neubig's shoulders weren't twitching then.

Within seconds, green-garbed technicians burst into the room. Dr. Neubig turned to me as they thrust the cart near Don. "Mrs. Aldrich, please excuse us."

I nodded, willing to let them do whatever they had to.

Someone guided me toward the door, past Don. I looked at him, his beautiful blue eyes wide-open and staring. "Good-bye, Donnie," I whispered.

In the hallway, the nurse asked if I needed to call anyone. Of course. We needed prayer. Still numb, I dialed the only number I could remember—that of my parents. Still feeling those celestial arms supporting me, I stammered to my dad and asked for immediate prayers.

I wouldn't be feeling God's tangible presence if Don was going to be all right. Those arms were supporting me for the news I was going to hear soon.

Then someone led me to the lounge, and I glanced back toward the scan room. Another crash cart had just arrived. Right behind it was Dr. Martin. At least Don wasn't alone.

They left me sitting on the sofa for just a moment, but soon another nurse patted me on the arm.

"He's going to be all right. Don't worry."

I stared at her. I wouldn't be feeling God's tangible presence if Don was going to be all right. Those arms were supporting me for the news I was going to hear soon.

Another woman was in the waiting room. With all of the commotion, she stood up and nervously looked down the hall.

"Something's wrong," she said.

I nodded. "It's my husband, ma'am."

Her stammered "oh" was filled with relief.

Within minutes Dr. Martin sat next to me. "Mrs. Aldrich, it's serious, but we're doing all we can."

I stared at him. "This is the preparation, isn't it? First you tell me how bad it is, then you'll tell me he's gone."

How vulnerable Dr. Martin seemed. "It *is* very bad. But we're trying to resuscitate him now."

Then he left. Resuscitate. They were trying to bring him *back*. I was wearing Don's watch from that morning when he had given it to me before his surgery. I watched the digital dial pulsate 2:22. What would he come back to? I'd seen and heard much in that room just now. If they brought him back, he'd have to go through that all over again. *Lord, I want Don*—but your will only. Your will only.

A tall man burst through the door and excitedly strode over to the woman near the window. "Boy, you oughta see what's happening down the hall," he said. "Somebody's in bad trouble."

His wife shushed him, whispering a hoarse, "It's that woman's husband."

Just then Dr. Neubig and Dr. Martin came in. I looked at those young faces. "He's gone, isn't he?"

They nodded.

I wanted to comfort them. "You know we both have a strong personal faith," I said, not realizing I hadn't used the past tense for Don. "I'm convinced the Lord showed mercy by taking him quickly now and sparing him worse things in the future."

Dr. Martin gripped my arm. "And you don't know the horrible things he was spared," he said. "You hang on to that in the days ahead."

Tumbling together were thoughts of Don's uncharacteristic personality traits and partial paralysis. On Nine North, I'd seen signs outside patient's rooms stating, "Patient is blind" but hadn't understood until that moment that Don's cancer would have destroyed the sight in those beautiful eyes. To push away the image of Don's being blind, I asked what had caused his death.

"Pulmonary embolus" was the immediate answer. At my questioning look, they offered the translation of "massive blood clots to the lungs." I thought of the partial lung I'd seen outlined on the screen and closed my eyes.

I had forms to sign and clothes to collect, so Dr. Martin walked with me back to the ward. Don's lunch tray was sitting on his table across the bed, waiting. A strangling sob escaped from deep within me. Don hadn't eaten that day. And never again would I hear my beloved Scotsman say, "Great meal, San."

* * *

The following days were a blur of somehow getting through them. Mother and Dad arrived at the hospital as I numbly folded Don's clothes and put them into his suitcase. I wanted it all to be just a terrible dream, but as we crossed the lobby near the scan room, the morgue personnel and a policeman were escorting Don's covered body into the service elevator. It was no dream.

At home I immediately told Jay and Holly. Jay searched my face, as though wondering if I was telling some terrible joke. Then he threw himself against me, sobbing. Holly just stared at me, her blank eyes betraying her incomprehension.

During the day, I made funeral arrangements. During the night, I stared into the shadows, remembering the sounds I'd heard when Don died.

By Friday noon, my Scotsman was at the funeral home. Now that the day had actually come, I moved in slow motion, unsure I had the strength to greet those who would visit. I wanted only to disappear, comfort my children and nurse my own pain.

Someone was moving cars in the drive. I didn't bother to see who it was because I didn't care. Any strength I once might have shown had evaporated with Don's last breath.

I stepped into the tub and turned the water on as far as it would go. If nothing else had come from Uncle Lawrence's death, I'd learned to be honest with God and myself about my sorrow. I put my head under the running water and sobbed.

"I hate this assignment, Lord. And I can't turn it back as I've done with writing projects that weren't right for me. I'm stuck with this one forever. Just please don't make me go through this alone; please stay close to us."

Sob after sob was swallowed by the water as it splashed onto my head, but Mother still heard and opened the door. Between her own sobs, she confessed she had asked the Lord last year to take her instead of Don. When her chest pains had started, she thought He was granting her request. I had no answer for her anguished cry of "Why didn't He?"

Exhausted, I picked up the washcloth, amazed at how heavy it was. How could I get through the days ahead? What had happened to the strength that had allowed me to stand between Don and the awful uncertainty before us?

* * *

As we stepped through the funeral home door, the greeter was carrying flowers down the hallway. The memory of Don's joy over the poinsettias on our hearth flashed across my mind.

Beyond the arch, Don was lying in the coffin I had chosen just the day before. I had been dreading that first viewing, but suddenly I wanted to be near my beloved Scotsman again. I gripped Jay and Holly's hands as together we walked toward him.

Neither child said anything, just stood quietly beside me, waiting to take their cue from me. For several minutes, I just looked at Donnie, remembering those long hours in the hospital, holding his hand, watching his breath come out through his lips in little puffs. I remembered how warm and sweet his breath had been upon my lips the day he reminded me the Lord never promised to give us an easy road. And I could almost hear him repeat a portion of the Twenty-third Psalm.

"Yea, though I walk through the valley of the shadow of death, I will fear no evil: for thou art with me."

I patted Don's shoulder, thinking of the struggle he had waged, and the grief we three would face without him.

"Ah, Donnie, you're free. You're free!" I whispered.

And from the other side of that valley, I'm sure he grinned at me.

Chapter Six

Since Then

August 1, 1989
Mount Kisco, New York

As difficult as it was to get through the days surrounding
Don's funeral, they were almost the easy part. For
months it took every bit of strength for me to accomplish
even the most basic chores. Because no one saw me running down the street shrieking, everyone assumed I was
doing well. No, I wasn't doing at all—but I was trying to
let the Lord do for me.

Philippians 4:19 was the Scripture Jay was memorizing
the day his dad died. The copied verse was on the kitchen
counter when I came home from the hospital to tell them
the bad news—as though the Lord himself offered special
comfort.

> "But my God shall supply all your need according to
> his riches in glory by Christ Jesus."

Many times I tested that promise, even occasionally challenging Him with "Even THIS need, God?" Gradually I learned that He hadn't overlooked anything. I learned to change the oil in the car and even—occasionally—balance the checkbook. But most of all I grew—learning much about myself and even more about my heavenly Father.

During the early months after Don's death, I felt as though my prayers weren't going any place. I was still talking to God but wasn't hearing answers the way I had during Don's struggle. Feeling spiritually abandoned, I demanded, "Why aren't you talking to me?"

Suddenly I thought of times when I had held an injured Jay or Holly on my lap. I hadn't talked, but had merely held them against my heart, surrounding hurt with love. Now that was what the Lord was doing for me. I was too hurt to listen to His plans for the future—I was capable of receiving only His comfort for that moment. In time, He would ease me off His lap and tenderly lead me to the tasks He planned. His silence hadn't meant He'd stopped caring.

During this time, I was determined that while Jay and Holly had lost their dad physically, they weren't going to lose me emotionally. Thus, every night as I tucked them in bed, I asked if they wanted to talk before we prayed together. Sometimes Jay shared a special memory of his dad or had a question about something at the funeral home. But not Holly. She still hadn't cried and kept all of her searing questions inside. As she prayed, her words were rote instead of from the heart.

Even as I continued to ask if she wanted to talk, she'd shake her head and turn away. Then one night, about two weeks after the funeral, she paused. "I do wonder one thing. When we prayed, didn't God listen?"

Oh, boy. With that one question, she'd galloped to the universal heart's cry.

Mentally I shot a quick prayer and then began the hardest explanation I've ever tried to give. We all compare ourselves to others; the trick is to get that comparison going in the right direction.

I reminded her of my Grandpa Ted who had died after his leg was severed in a Kentucky coal mine. He was only 22 years old and left three children under the age of four. I reminded her of a 28-year-old man who had been killed at the corner light just the week before. His wife was pregnant with a child he would never hold. Then I talked about God's gift to us of those extra 16 months when the doctors thought her daddy would die within weeks. I added that he could have died with the first cancer in 1977 when she had been only three years old.

When I was talked out, I asked if she felt like praying that night. She nodded, then began. "Thank you, God, that Daddy died now instead of when I was little."

I didn't hear much of the rest of her prayer. She was only eight years old.

* * *

As I analyze all that's happened in these past few years, I confess I'm a different—perhaps even better—person because of the traumas. Not only do I see the hurts of others now, but I've learned to embrace the joy in *this* moment.

The Pharaoh wall hanging was thrown into a drawer the afternoon of December 29, 1982. For years I couldn't look at it; the memory of my failure to finish it for my beloved clown was still too painful. Then on the fifth anniversary of Don's death, I answered Jay's question of "Whatever happened to that needlepoint?" by hauling it out again. As I picked up the gold metallic thread, it was as though I'd tossed everything into the drawer just the week before. But then I realized my eyes had deteriorated so much I had trouble threading the needle. . . . If nothing else, their weakened condition emphasized how long Don has been dead.

> *I'm a different—perhaps even better—person because of the traumas. Not only do I see the hurts of others now, but I've learned to embrace the joy in* this *moment.*

The Pharaoh is now framed and in our home, no longer a painful memory but a symbol of my life—awkward and full of mistakes, crooked stitches and bumpy knots—but still containing beauty and strength.

Marta Gabre-Tsadick's book, *Sheltered by the King,* was published three months after Don died. She and her husband Deme Telke-Wold continue to be my treasured friends. Knowing them has not only made my world larger, but their work with the Ethiopian refugees has helped me put my own grief in perspective.

* * *

Studies show that the stress caused by the loss of a spouse can produce enormous physical problems. As much as I dislike fitting into a pattern, I became one of those statistics. Within the first year after Don's death, I developed lupus—a virulent cousin to arthritis and an attacker of the immune system. After I'd gotten over my irritation that my body had betrayed my lack of inner strength, my brown rice program went back into gear.

Much of what I'd learned while trying to help Don proved exactly what I needed to fight my own physical illness.

After Don died, I taught for the rest of that school year—undoubtedly a mistake. I needed to allow myself to crawl away to lick my deep wounds, but I had an image to uphold. A few days after Don died, mutual friends asked Carl, my "big brother" co-worker, how long I'd be off from teaching. He said I'd be out just a week—that I was strong. Strong? How could I be strong when my entire world had just collasped?

The best thing I did was take a personal leave that following year—after 15 years of teaching. The worst part of that decision was telling our relatives. They didn't know the hours I'd prayed for direction as I fought my fears—both for the future and in facing their opinions.

Looking back makes it easy to say, "Well, of course I was supposed to leave the classroom." But in those early days I felt as though I was jumping off Rebel Rock. Every Southern town with a cliff also has a Civil War legend of the young Confederate messenger chased by Yankees. Rather than being taken prisoner, he ran at breakneck speed toward the rocky cliff and—with a triumphant rebel yell—threw himself onto the rocks below. (Whether or not a horse is included in the story depends upon the story-teller's love for animals.)

For me to leave teaching after 15 years of security felt as traumatic as being chased by Yankees. But in shaky faith I took a deep breath, leaped off into the abyss—and stepped onto God's hands. I took long walks in the morning—finally allowing myself time to begin the healing. But best of all, I was available to my children. I went on every field trip, attended every class party and grinned from the fifth row at each school presentation.

Don had had our wills drawn up within a week of his

first hospital release. But while I was thankful for his careful planning, I also thought of other widows suddenly thrust into an unwanted job while wading through raw grief. As I worried about them, I became convinced that the greatest thing the church can do for a widow is help her stay home with her children for a while longer. They don't need to be on the church books forever—just long enough to regroup emotionally.

During my time off from teaching, I felt the Lord was preparing me for a new career. Excitement mingled with fear as I determined to be open to whatever He had for me. But even as I sensed God's hand upon my life, I still missed my beloved clown. Even the most ordinary experiences stirred up vast longings to have him with us. I missed his booming laugh and his lighthearted way of disciplining Jay and Holly, but gradually I took over that duty with resignation and—sometimes—determination.

And I conquered that awful self-propelled lawn mower. The first summer after his death, I had to move the bushes along the side fence to protect them from my wild mower manuevers. As I plunged the shovel into the soil beneath their roots, I imagined Don's reaction. (I'm not convinced those who have died can watch us. After all, how can it truly be heaven if they have to watch our fumblings?) But if Don could see me, surely he elbowed Uncle Lawrence and said, "See that? I complained about those bushes for years, but as soon as *she* had to mow around them, they're moved the first week."

* * *

In my naivete, I'd said to a few close friends that I was giving myself three years off from the world—one year to heal (boy, was that naive), one year to make decisions and the final year to act upon them. Yet I knew a major chapter of my life was finished and I trusted the Lord to lead me into the next phase. I took Bible classes and attended the community Bible study at my church, sometimes even having the privilege of teaching it. And, of course, my writing gradually increased.

In my naivete, I'd said to a few close friends that I was giving myself three years off from the world—one year to heal (boy, was that naive), one year to make decisions and the final year to act upon them.

Then one of my friends, Tom Rost, president of the Detroit- based R. G. and G. R. Harris Funeral Homes, Inc.—and the one who had directed Don's funeral—asked me to join his staff as Community Service Representative. Concerned for the many grieving families he served, Tom had invited a counselor, Dr. John Canine, director of Maximum Living in Birmingham, Michigan, to help. My position supported his work. Using his outlines, I gave grief seminars at churches, hospitals, service organizations and schools. When the space shuttle Challenger exploded, teachers invited me to speak about grief to their classes.

Of course, many audiences were uncomfortable as I was introduced (after all, I was from a *funeral* home). So I tried to put them at ease by saying, "Community Service Representative. Isn't that classy? My boss picked that title because he didn't like the one I suggested. I'd offered to lose weight and call myself 'The Slim Reaper.'"

Groaning laughter followed, but my audience listened. Death is one of those subjects we don't want to talk about because we don't want to face immortality. The thought of lying cold and still under the ground is too awful to think about— until we lose someone we love. And then we can't talk enough about it, but no one wants to listen. I'm amazed at the people who just need someone to hear their pain. I'm sure I never saw them before I had the same need. Don and I had asked God to bring His good out of our trauma, but neither of us could have guessed that grief counseling would be part of His answer.

And while I was struggling with my own adjustments to raising two children by myself, another grief came swooping in; I learned that the family of long-ago friends had been destroyed by the mother's alcoholism. As I tried to make sense of the madness, I worked with Jim Broome, co-founder of Alcoholics for Christ. Not only did I learn much about what had happened in their lives, but I suddenly understood the childhood dynamics produced by my relatives' drinking. That enlightenment would have been enough, but once we give a situation to the Lord, He never leaves it half-finished. As I wrote about alcoholism, Dean Merrill, then editor of *Christian Herald* magazine not only purchased my article "What Makes Alcoholics Stop?" but invited me to interview for an opening on his editorial staff. Jay, Holly and I flew to New York as a lark; without a degree in journalism I knew I'd never be offered the job. Wrong. Within a week, the three of us were back in New York and starting the next new chapter of our lives.

Occasionally some well-meaning person will see only my strength and murmur, "You've certainly got it all together." No, I don't. But I'm trying to let God hold it all together. And that's all any of us can do while we're waiting to rejoin our beloved clowns.

Book Two

Legacy of My Clown

CHAPTER ONE

Turning Grief into Good

My identity revolved around Don, so it was—and is—only because of Jesus that I continue with this thing loosely called "life." In the process, I've learned that all of us lose something precious at one time or another. I wish I were the *last* widow. Not only would others be spared pain, but everybody would say, "Oh, you poor dear." But *everybody* hurts. Even those who haven't lost through death (yet) or divorce have lost in other significant ways. Prisoners grieve the loss of their freedom, transferees grieve leaving friends and familiar surroundings, adults grieve for their youth and patients grieve over lost body parts.

After one of my seminars, a pastor asked, "How can I get my people over their grief?" He was relieved to hear that getting people *over* grief isn't his job—helping them *through* it is.

Our bodies are constructed in such a way that we must grieve. And if we aren't allowed to grieve appropriately, we will express it inappropriately, often through anger or depression.

Let's define two important terms:

Bereavement is the time after a major loss. Its outer signs, such as wearing black or having annual memorial services, are set by our society.

Grief is the emotional response and can stay with us for years. But a thin line exists between grieving the loss of someone we love and grieving the way our life has turned out. We all know people who are caught in that early grief even years later; they're difficult to be around because no one can help them.

Of course I knew the widow's special pain all too well, but while I agreed that Don's death was an amputation, I had decided it didn't always have to bleed.

When I worked for the funeral home, part of my job was encouraging new widows. Of course I knew the widow's special pain all too well, but while I agreed that Don's death was an amputation, I had decided it didn't always have to bleed. Most women found comfort in my soothing, "It may always hurt, but it won't always hurt *this* much."

Then one of the women brought her friend Georgia to the widows' group. Georgia sobbed throughout the introductions. Then after she told her story, I nodded comfortingly as I asked, "How long has it been?"

"Nineteen years!" was her sobbing answer.

Nineteen years? She wasn't grieving for her husband, she was dealing with unresolved issues—including guilt. Nothing I said unstuck her. She had decided long ago that she would remain miserable for the rest of her life.

* * *

Same Sorrow, Different Reactions

The grieving process is complicated by individual forces but the intensity with which we grieve depends upon a combination of four variables: the closeness of the relationship and whether the death was sudden, premature or violent. Any one of these makes our grief intense, but with each additional characteristic, our emotional pain deepens.

Closeness of the relationship
This normally applies to spouse, children, siblings or parents, but can include distant relatives if a special bond was shared—such as I had with Uncle Lawrence.

Profound grief also occurs when a close friend dies. After Don's death, our friend Gail Collins asked her Sunday School class to pray for me. Later a woman touched her arm, "And I'm praying for you too, dear." That simple statement gave Gail permission to cry, releasing pain.

Sudden Death
How many times do we hear of the death of someone and we say, "But I just saw him yesterday morning!"

If cancer holds any redeeming factor, it's the time it gives us to think about death. This feeling, called "anticipatory grief," begins as soon as the doctor pronounces the diagnosis.

Premature Death
We tend to think of a child or young adult when we hear of "premature death." But the term can be aptly applied to those much older. We all know people who go to the doctor on Tuesday for the annual check-up and hear, "You're

the healthiest 77-year-old I've ever seen." And then he drops dead on Friday. That's premature, and the widow doesn't want to hear that he had a good life. The phrase carries no healing until *she* can say it.

My friend Mrs. Doan was 94 when she received word that her 96-year-old sister had died after going to Hollywood to live with her grandson. Mrs. Doan sadly commented, "I just know all that wild living shortened her life." (May *my* life be shortened at 96 by "wild" living!) But Mrs. Doan knew her sister was looking forward to a marvelous party on her one-hundredth birthday. In that sense, the death was indeed "premature."

Violent Death

Whether it's murder, suicide, horrible accident or war, we can't stand suffering. When I worked for an Army ROTC unit during the Vietnam War, our officers were often called on to tell parents their son had been killed. The stunned silence usually was broken first by the question, "Did he suffer?" Our officers usually didn't have that information, but one of them always replied, "It was quick. Very quick."

Each of these grief intensifiers carries its own pain, and each additional one adds that much more. Of course we feel sorrow when the 89-year-old grandmother dies, but if she had been ill for a long time and died peacefully in her sleep, we come to terms with the loss fairly quickly. But our sorrow isn't always so neatly handed to us. What do we do when the sorrow comes wrapped in a close friendship and is sudden, premature *and* violent?

In my 15 years of high school teaching in Garden City, Michigan, I lost many of my students. Seventeen-year-old Greg was murdered in a senseless robbery at the gas station he managed. Tim was 17 when his leg was amputated because of cancer. He died only months later. Brilliant Steve would have been 35 this year, but he remains in my heart as the eternal 18-year-old who fell several stories at his college parking ramp.

I remember handsome 15-year-old Jim in his jean jacket, grinning and saying, "Hey, I'm OK, Mrs. A." just before he went home to take the top of his head off with a shotgun blast. Rosie was 14 years old when a car on Ford Road slammed into her. Vietnam took not only 3 of my schoolmates but 16 of Garden City's students. I remember their grace on the football field or shyness in asking the girl in English class to the prom—and I hurt.

Sometimes the victories are small by themselves; it's only in the comparison of how we used *to be that the miracle is seen. For even the most tragic loss can be turned into good—if we'll allow it to be.*

Suicide, war, murder, accident—death often is absolutely senseless—and even my Presbyterian refuge of the sovereignty of God doesn't offer a satisfactory explanation. How tired our heavenly Father must be of our blaming Him for the consequences of human decision! I've finally settled that our only choice in the midst of tragedy isn't whether or not we'll go through it, but *how.* Only the Lord's presence offers comfort—and the hope that we will see our loved ones again.

Turning Tragedy into Triumph

The title of this chapter is "Turning Grief into Good," but

how do we accomplish that when the loss is so senseless? Granted, sometimes the victories are small by themselves; it's only in the comparison of how we *used* to be that the miracle is seen. For even the most tragic loss *can* be turned into good—if we'll allow it to be. Some people start support groups to reach out to others. Some fight the things that took their child: Candy Lightner co-founded Mothers Against Drunk Drinking (M.A.D.D.) after her 13-year-old daughter was killed.

Making New Discoveries
The good doesn't have to be dramatic. Through Don's death, I've discovered I have strength I'd never recognized. And my heart is larger toward others. An enormous number of hurting folks are out there—folks I never would have seen if it hadn't been for my own pain. And I played the "tough guy" game long enough to know that often behind the toughest, strongest exterior is the biggest hurt.

Living One Day at a Time
We can also turn tragedy into good by learning to live one day at a time. That's what cancer taught us. Don and I learned that *today* is precious—not next year. We also learned that the worth of property and antiques faded right out when compared to what we already had in our children and in each other.

Looking at Our Own Mortality
After Don's death, I also was forced to look at my own mortality. Suddenly I understood my Kentucky grandmother's long- ago admonishment: "Honey, none of us was put here to stay." Somehow, I never believed that until Don was lying cold and silent against the satin pillow. If clowns can die, then we all will.

Counting Our Blessings

But even as far as I've been brought by the Lord in these seven years, special occasions—such as baptism or graduations—bring fresh pain. No one moves from despair to emotional recovery in a straight line—no matter what level of grief we're dealing with. Grief comes in waves. Just about the time we take a deep breath and say, "OK, I can get through this," we get hit again.

The spring following Don's death, Jay and Holly were helping me clean out the garage. On the bottom shelf we found their dad's old, ratty golf shoes I'd demanded he throw away. He'd stood in the sunshine on a long-ago Saturday morning and grinned in his little-boy way that let me know he'd do whatever *he* wanted with them.

And there I was months later, holding the shoes without Don and without the sunshine, and crying both at the memory and the knowledge I'd never again hear his "Ahh, San." But I have been blessed by the love of a good man and that memory helps me over many of the rough spots.

CHAPTER TWO

Moving Through Grief

By labeling the four major stages of grief, I'm not trying to pigeonhole people, but help them through a confusing, frightening time. We don't move through those stages in precise order, however. Not only does grief come in waves, but it's influenced by feelings of abandonment, guilt and emotional struggles with other family members. Just when we think we can handle the situation, we are reminded of our loss, and the emotional pain swells again. And we don't move from one point to another in a straight line. At times we'll move back and forth from one stage to another—especially in the latter stages.

Dr. Elisabeth Kübler-Ross found that the *dying* work through five basic stages: denial, anger, bargaining, depression and acceptance.[1] We now know that the *families* of the terminally ill go through these stages too.

But after the death, the griever faces still more adjustments that usually fall into one of four major categories: numbness, searching, disorientation and resolution.

Numbness

Numbness can last from just a few hours to several weeks. Everything seems to move in slow motion, causing the griever to feel as though he's in a bad dream or walking through a fog.

During this stage, intense grief may produce chest pains or feelings of suffocation. Don had trouble breathing the morning before he died, so after his death my mind translated his suffering into my own shortness of breath. But since I knew what was happening, I wore v-neck blouses, instead of my usual bow ones, and waited for the smothering sensation to pass. Within a couple of weeks, my breathing was back to normal.

Drastic weight gains or losses can occur during the early stages of grief. Since grieving takes enormous physical strength, it isn't unusual to lose weight even without trying. When the body has worked through the initial trauma and is getting ready to rejoin life, the weight is often regained without a change in eating habits.

Massive weight gains can also occur. Often people stuff their emotions by overdosing on high calories. One gal complained that she had gained 20 pounds the first month after her husband's death. They had always taken a walk together after dinner. Not only had she lost the motivation to take the walk, but she was trying to soothe her pain by eating childhood comfort foods of chocolate cake and cream horns.

Searching

Searching—the next stage—can be an intense time as the griever comes out of the fog and asks, "What happened?

How did he die?" In the early part of this stage, she'll want to see the autopsy report or police account. Not only is it normal, but healthy. Dr. John Canine often explains this stage with the statement "lack of control and lack of understanding result in enormous emotional turmoil." Getting our questions answered, painful though it is, gives us some emotional control.

The later part of the stage often produces a literal searching. After Don's death, I traveled to Europe and, later, to the Middle East, making up for the years he didn't want to leave Michigan. And, in every country, I caught myself scanning the crowds for my bearded Scotsman. That's even after I had seen him die. How much worse the searching must be for those who don't have their questions answered.

Perhaps you're thinking, "That's dumb. My husband died and I didn't struggle during this stage. I read the autopsy report and that was that." I'm happy for you. And I confess that I envy you too. But some of us had to work through childhood emotional baggage—rejection, low self-esteem and feelings of abandonment— while trying to cope with regular grieving. For us, the searching stage is much longer.

Questions

During this stage, that awful question Why? surfaces. Often it's accompanied by "What else could I have done?" or "Should he have stayed on the chemotherapy?" or "Should he have gotten off the chemotherapy?" Of course this is a painful time for those *listening* to the griever's questions too. No quick answers exist. After Peter Marshall's funeral, his anguished widow, Catherine, asked her mother why this had happened. Her mother, also a widow, answered quietly, "In God's time, He will give you his

answers." With hindsight we see the ministry the Lord
gave Catherine because of her grief. Countless people
have been comforted by writings that could not have been
produced except through her own suffering.

Comparisons

This time of searching is a crucial stage for those grieving
over a child. Suddenly the "perfect" child has died, adding
an additional emotional burden to the other children:
"Sharon wouldn't have left her room in such a mess."
"Sharon wouldn't have slapped her brother." "Sharon
wouldn't have brought home a paper like this."

Obviously enormous repercussions catapult throughout the family unless they understand what is happening.
It's important the children especially understand that their
mother is *not* saying she wishes another of her children
had died in Sharon's place. She's merely reminding herself
that Sharon was a special person with many good
qualities—thus giving credibility to her own grief.

Often the griever so needs to remind herself and others of the deceased's special qualities that she may tend to
deify him, ignoring his irritating traits. She'll say, "If ever a
saint walked around, he was it." Or, "I'll never find anyone
as good as he was." This can be tough to listen to, especially if you remember only the deceased's less desirable
qualities. For the first six months, survivors need to concentrate on all of the good qualities for these add validity to
that special loss. Then we can start looking at the whole
person.

The old joke says the pastor asked the rhetorical question, "Can any of us say we are perfect? If you are, stand
up right now."

One man in the fifth row stood up. The pastor was
astounded. "Are you perfect?"

"No, I'm not," the man replied. "I'm just standing on behalf of my wife's *first* husband."

Guilt

Guilt will be a major problem during this stage. The best way to dispel it is by expressing it. Before I worked with Dr. Canine, I thought guilt was the plain old vanilla type that made us visit relatives when we were already up to our eyebrows in work. But I've since learned three guilts exist: true, false and misplaced.

True guilt. This guilt shows up when we've done something wrong and we need to say, "I'm sorry." This is the avenue God uses to remind us we need to ask for His forgiveness. But when it's tacked onto grief, it can have a deep hold. Dr. Canine tells about the couple who were in the middle of a shouting match when the husband grabbed his heart and fell over. His last words to his wife were curses. Some memory, huh? And she's stuck with the guilt of having started the whole thing by not wanting to go fishing with him to begin with. How does she get unstuck so she can stop beating herself emotionally and get on with her life?

Two simple ways—write a letter or send a message through a prayer. Of course the letter can't be sent (although some people "mail" them by burning them in the fireplace), but it's therapeutic just to express all those things you wish you could say. "I'm sorry. Please forgive me" are five of the most cleansing words in our language. Having the griever express on paper or to an empty chair all those searing thoughts are effective tactics every counselor knows.

The same healing comes when we send a message

through our prayer. A simple apology offers release from tormenting thoughts.

One of my friends tells how stricken she was when a particular elderly widower in their church died. Just a few weeks earlier she'd requested that he postpone his frequent calls until later in the evening; he called several times just as she was preparing dinner for her family. He never called again.

In the rush of her schedule, she forgot about him—until he died. For the next several days she gave herself pep talks emphasizing how busy her large family kept her and how rude he had been to call during her busiest time of the day. The guilt remained.

Finally one evening she knelt by her bed and said through her tears, "Please tell him I'm sorry." Peace finally arrived—along with a new sensitivity.

* * *

False guilt. This guilt—and the next—are two of Satan's favorite tools to torment the griever. False guilt is exactly that—false. It's expressed most often through phrases such as "I should have." *I should have insisted he stay on chemotherapy.* Or, *I should have insisted he stop chemotherapy. I should have done more.*

Several years ago, dear neighbors were involved in an automobile accident just before Christmas. Everyone survived, but the 8-year-old daughter had to have extensive operations on her foot. Two days after the accident, I drove the father to the nearby town, where his insurance adjuster had totaled out the van. On the way there, he kept saying, "It's all my fault. If only we'd stayed home. We had no business going."

He needed more than a listener; he needed direction.

"Look," I said, "what if you'd stayed home, and she'd gotten hurt? Wouldn't you be saying, 'We should have gone'? What you're feeling right now is so common that counselors even have a name for it—false guilt. *You* didn't cut her foot. That happened when the van hit a patch of ice."

Relief swept over his face. Then we could talk about the distortion guilt brings to any situation, especially to the parent who feels as though he should always protect his family. We can't spend our lives in a basement; we have to be involved in daily activities that all have the potential for danger. Besides, even if we hid in the basement, we'd have to deal with the guilt over our child's rickets from lack of sunshine.

My neighbor was able to verbalize his pain to someone who could help put it in the proper perspective. But if it isn't acknowledged, it grows. Another friend had an accident that resulted in her father's death. Her own injuries kept her from attending his funeral but not from dwelling on the tragedy. A year later, she sobbed to me, "I killed my dad."

In her family, life's traumas weren't discussed, they were merely borne. But this hurt was too great for her to carry alone. For over an hour, I talked about the various guilts, stressing she hadn't killed her father. But even reminders that he wouldn't want her punishing herself made no difference as she kept saying, "No, I killed him."

Finally I asked her to pray in her own language, ask for God's help and send a message to her father. I couldn't understand the words but I understood the emotion. When she looked up from the prayer, I took her hands into mine. "How did your father die?"

She looked at me, bewildered. Hadn't she been explaining his death for the last hour? But suddenly recognition flooded her face and she answered, "He died in an auto accident" instead of "I killed him." She had taken the first step toward healing.

Misplaced guilt. Guilt of this nature occurs when a normal situation explodes out of proportion. Years ago, before Easter flowers were sold in the local variety stores, Carl always ordered a corsage for Beverly. But one Easter they had been so busy with parenting a new baby and purchasing their first home that he forgot—until Easter morning. Slapping his forehead in frustration, he apologized repeatedly. Beverly had laughed, saying it didn't matter. But two weeks later, when she was killed in an automobile accident, it mattered very much. The forgotten flowers tormented Carl.

Decision-Making
Decision-making during this searching stage can be catastrophic too. I remembered the universal advice that those who are grieving shouldn't make any major decisions for the first year. Like it or not, we *aren't* thinking clearly. So I didn't think about moving, refused offers for our Maranatha mobile home and kept the children in their same school. All I had to do was coast for a while—or so I thought. Then the engine went out on the station wagon. Soon I was sending my own prayer apologies.

Don had always decided not only what type of car we'd buy, but how often. My choice was whether or not I wanted to drive it. Suddenly I had to figure out how to buy a car *and* how to pay for it. I casually talked to friends about their experiences, trying not to sound desperate. But no matter how much I listened or how much I read, the final, scary decision was mine—alone. I even asked my trusted mechanic to rebuild the engine, so I could postpone the decision. But he refused, saying the car had too many other things wrong with it. So began my search. More than once, my prayers ended with an earnest "Please tell Don I'm sorry. And please show me which car to buy."

Out of one prayer came the idea to list what I needed in a vehicle, thus narrowing my decision. It had to have four doors, a trunk that could haul my ironing board back and forth to Maranatha and enough engine power to pass a coal truck in the Kentucky mountains. (I've never claimed logic as one of my strong points.)

At last I settled on a gray, American-made sedan with a V-6 engine—our Detroit expressways didn't need the coal-truck passing gear after all. In retrospect, the total process was rather melodramatic, but that happens when decision-making is new to us. If nothing else, the trauma made me all the more determined to teach Jay and Holly how to go through the process less painfully.

Disorientation

Disorientation can be scary. In this stage we come to grips with the idea we must go on with our life. But the only way we can hang on to the one we lost is by looking backward. Trying to move in two directions at once can result in depression, unless we control the pace.

Old Possessions
It's during disorientation that closets are cleaned out, clothes given to the Salvation Army and tools and golf clubs to sons or best friends. To do that before the griever is ready can complicate the letting-go process. Three days after the funeral, Don's dad tried to convince me to clean out the closet before he returned to Florida. Never had I argued with him, but that day I quietly refused.

He countered with what made sense to him. "You have to get rid of those things that remind you of him."

I dug my heels in. "If I do that, I'll have to get rid of everything—including his clock collection and Jay and Holly! No. When I'm ready, I'll sort through his things. And not until then."

And not giving in was exactly the best thing I could have done for myself. Not only did I gain some control over my immediate future, but I also dared to tell someone what I needed. Of course it hurt to see Don's clothes hanging next to mine every morning when I opened the closet, but it also helped me adjust gradually to the fact he wasn't coming back. I finally gave away his clothing in March—three months later—and only when *I* was ready.

It used to be the practice of some church groups to discard the deceased's personal items while the family attended the funeral. How awful! Isn't it amazing the emotional pain well- meaning friends can inflict?

* * *

All personal items fall into two categories: *linking objects* and *mementos.*

Linking objects. These objects include personal items, such as toothbrushes, and should be discarded quickly. For years, our green ceramic toothbrush holder in the main bath held four brushes. After Don's death, the empty spot bothered me more than if I'd left his toothbrush there, so I added a different colored one for my evening brushing. Another widow solved that same dilemma by adding a toothbrush for granddaughter's visits.

Sometimes the linking objects are a bit more bizarre. At one of my seminars, a woman asked about her sister insisting upon sleeping on her husband's pillow because it still had his body scent on it. I assured her that in time the scent would fade and common sense and hygiene would force her to wash the material. But until then, it was normal for her to want to hang onto that smell just a bit longer.

A linking object can even be a room arrangement. Again, that change must come when the griever is ready for it. It took 15 months before I was ready to rearrange our bedroom, taking down the single bed that had been mine for almost a year and a half and returning to the double bed Don and I had shared all those years before his cancer. After his death, I had found it less traumatic to ignore the big bed—and the resulting clutter—and continue sleeping in my single bed.

But suddenly one overcast morning, I decided it was time to turn the bedroom from "ours" into "mine," and I tackled the chore with determination. About an hour into the job, the phone rang. It was my mother.

"You sound out of breath," she said. "Did you have to run up the stairs to answer?"

"No. Jay and I were just shoving furniture around. I've taken down the single bed and was rearranging my bedroom."

Suddenly she was quietly crying.

"What's wrong?"

No answer. Just more sniffs.

"Mother, please don't. You know I can't stand it when you cry long distance. I'm only rearranging furniture."

More sniffs came, but gradually she could talk. "It's just that the Lord answered my prayer. When I was over there two weeks ago and helped you fold the laundry, I looked at that crowded room and asked the Lord to help you move on. And every morning for two weeks, I've asked Him to nudge you to rearrange that room."

That startled me, of course, but also got me to thinking. What if she had marched in and announced, "OK, now you've ignored this room long enough. It's time to get on with your life." Obviously it wouldn't have worked.

* * *

Mementos. These include family pictures and heirlooms and are an important part of the family's memories. Mementos—such as pictures—should be kept. The family portrait that we had taken just two months before Don's death is still hanging in our upstairs hallway. Few people have seen it. But those who have don't comment on it. Undoubtedly, they didn't want to "remind" me of what I've lost, but their silence hurts far more. Even something as bland as, "What a lovely picture. I know you treasure it" would be carried in my heart for days.

On the other hand, some mementos may cause more pain than joy. Don had won a number of golf and tennis trophies, which I dusted for two years after his death. When I finally decided I needed the shelf space for books, I asked my friend Janet Wears to help me clean the family room that day. Painful though it was, it was time to pack away both the object and the memory.

I did the same with the wedding pictures hanging in antique frames in the upstairs hallway. After my trip to the Middle East in 1985, I replaced the shots of the nervous young couple taken 19 years ago with pictures of me at Masada and on the Nile River. The trip symbolized my acceptance of my widowhood and my reluctant willingness to move on with my life.

Mementos also include the clothing. When I was finally ready to go through Don's clothes, I asked Jay and Holly if they had special items they wanted me to keep for them.

They both chose several sports jerseys to wear with jeans. I also put aside Don's varsity jacket with his tennis letter. In the spring of 1988, Jay—then 15—discovered it and tried it on. It fit perfectly. He wore it for the rest of the semester, quietly marveling at his 1959 treasure.

I also saved Don's expensive sweaters to give to Jay. With the family's Scottish background, how could I do otherwise? It was only when he wore them the *first* time that I thought of his dad's having worn them.

New Realizations

It was during this time I was ready to remember Don as a whole person—including his intense competitiveness, even when playing a board game and his insistence upon handling all family finances. Not everyone was comfortable with my honesty. When a new friend asked me to describe Don, I mentioned his booming laugh, his love for others, his delight in filling our home with company. Then I added, "But he wasn't a saint."

My friend, not realizing the emotional step that admission represented for me, was horrified. "How can you say that about your husband? Don't you have any respect for his memory?"

I let her rant, secure in my new confidence.

A normal statement also made during this time is, "I'll never marry again." At the time the widow says it, she really means it. That's part of her need to deify the one she's lost, thereby reminding herself that he was so special she can never have that kind of love again.

And she won't. Even if she remarries the following year, the circumstances are different— families may be combined, careers may be changed—and life's realities have replaced her wide-eyed glow. But sooner or later, trying to remain married to a dead spouse doesn't work.

At the time I'm writing this, it's been almost seven years since Don's death, but I haven't started dating yet. Not only am I too chicken-hearted to jump back into that sweaty-palms stage, but I haven't seen enough happy second marriages to make me want to add a husband to my already hectic life. As long as I remain unmarried, I have the privilege of following only the Lord's directions. I'm enjoying raising my two teenagers and have an exciting career that's directly from the Lord. I'm not ready to subject either myself or my children to another major adjustment. Yes, you may remind me of this when you hear I've nailed my navy blue suit jacket to my office door and run away with a banjo-playing gypsy.

But sooner or later, trying to remain married to a dead spouse doesn't work.

But even as I'm arguing with myself, I remember a startling realization 18 months after Don died. Jay, Holly, my parents and I attended the Gun and Musket Show at Greenfield Village in Dearborn, Michigan and enjoyed historical enactments by folks dressed to match the time period of their firearms.

As I ambled across the village green toward the Civil War recruitment tent, a ruggledly handsome Old West Cavalry officer strode toward us. From his black hat to his polished black boots, he personified masculinity. I was so taken by the sight, I breathed, "Oh, my!" without thinking. Apparently, he could read lips—or eyes—because he smiled in that slow, knowing way I hadn't seen since college and veered toward me.

Immediately I averted my eyes and scurried to catch up with my family. As I did so, a new sadness, as well as a new awareness, wrapped itself around me: My husband was dead, but I wasn't.

In the following weeks, that realization made me withdraw even more from my friends as I sorted through thoughts about my future—including a recent contact by a former boyfriend. And I made the decision my wedding rings would stay on my hand as a symbol of Isaiah 54:5: "For thy Maker is thine husband." With those hurdles crossed, I was free to rebuild my life—following only the Lord's direction. I was also free from the temptation to walk into a gathering and glance around, wondering who was there.

Resolution

Resolution signals the beginning of rejoining life. Joy—even laughter—returns. I felt guilty the first time I laughed after Don died even though it was because of a wild family story my brother, Mitch, told. How could I laugh when Don was lying in Oak Grove Cemetery?

Laughter Restored

Throughout our marriage, my humor rarely emerged because life was serious stuff. I even occasionally accused Don of not taking things seriously enough. Still he taught me how to laugh not only at life's quirks but even at myself.

After he died, I decided I could never laugh again without the example of his own booming laugh. But then as I moved through my grief, I noticed the preciousness of each moment. Don's laughter had drawn people to him, including Jay and Holly. I would either laugh again or I would have to disappear.

Even with that decision, my reentry into the world

came gradually. Perhaps the discovery of my lupus made me decide I was going to enjoy my children while I could. Or maybe the realization came when I worked on the funeral home staff with Dr. Canine and saw the healing that laughter produced.

Medically, laughter causes the brain to release enzymes called "endorphins," thus relieving pain. Norman Cousins used this concept in battling a rare connective tissue disease by watching Three Stooges movies. When Proverbs says, "A merry heart doeth good like a medicine" (17:22) it's true!

Somewhere in the midst of my grieving, I gave myself permission to laugh. Those who didn't know me during my intense stage can't believe laughter was ever foreign to me. When anything strikes me as funny now, my laughter bounces off the walls. How soon laughter or even quiet grins return to our lives depends upon how intense were the circumstances causing our grief. But a time comes when we must make a decision to allow the laughter to return—and thus rejoin life—or pull our gloom even tighter around our shoulders.

Living Renewed

Resolution also comes when the griever says to himself, "Life goes on." One of our neighbors, Bill Fife, had taught with Don for 16 years, so he often gave me reports of the school's continuing activity. Then he'd add that I had to get on with my life too. More than once I thought, *If he says, "Life goes on" one more time, I'll smack him.* Life *does* go on—but I needed to wade through all of the emotions until I could say it to myself.

As we work through our grief, the lines between the stages often blur—especially between disorientation and resolution. I miss Don terribly and still hurt as I think about all he went through. But I knew I was moving into resolution in 1984 when I decided to go to Oberammergau, Germany to see the 350th anniversary of the Passion Play.

Don had said in 1980 I could attend the next one, but after he died, I struggled over that. Was it right for the three of us to go when he couldn't? And even though we were going with our church group, would people think I was "The Merry Widow"?

As I thought and prayed about it, I realized I was going to be miserable no matter what choice I made. If we stayed home, I'd be unhappy knowing I was "supposed" to be in Europe. If we went, I'd be miserable knowing Don was "supposed" to be with us. Finally I decided if I was going to be miserable anyway, I'd rather be miserable in Europe!

That decision proved to be the best one. Our group landed in Milano, Italy as the first stop in our two-week adventure of seeing places previously available to me only through classroom textbooks and travel magazines. But none of that would have been mine unless I had given myself permission to enjoy life again.

During resolution a creative surge appears. Not only does the survivor begin or intensify journal entries, but she will often look for ways to bring good out of her suffering. Some parents start support groups, actively reaching out as they hear of tragedies.

Some find peace in volunteer work. When Don was in the hospital that final time, one of the most helpful volunteers was a widow who remembered her own long days of sitting by a hospital bed during the holidays. She anticipated my needs and outlined the schedule of several of the departments.

After Jay and Holly are grown, I hope to help in an

understaffed ward at holidays too. But for now my creativity has come through a grasp of *this moment's* joy. Now when I take a walk on a glorious summer day, I count the various shades of green. My record is 14.

The intense person I used to be couldn't see beauty as long as carpets remained unvacuumed and articles untyped. But the person I am now has learned how fragile life is and looks for the healing of wonderful things around me. If something is funny, I laugh. If the sunset is incredible, I comment on it.

> *The person I am now has learned how fragile life is and looks for the healing of wonderful things around me. If something is funny, I laugh. If the sunset is incredible, I comment on it.*

Oh, I still have my moments of wanting it to be June 1977—before Don's first cancer—but I'm enough of a realist to accept the loss of our position as the perfect American family. Those days can't be called back. I can only grow from those experiences and help others cope with the losses heading their way. Of course that acceptance of reality doesn't stop my longing to have Don see Jay shaving every day and Holly in her eighth-grade graduation dress, but it's time for me to rejoin life.

Liberty Regained

During resolution, the griever may feel a responsibility to give her friends permission to stop grieving. Don's golfing buddies at Maranatha gave a missionary fund-raising tournament in his name for six summers, starting in 1983. The money raised provided wells in Bangladesh, air-strip equipment in the jungles of Bolivia, helped a prison ministry in Quito, Ecuador and paid for a translation of Genesis for a South American tribe.

I treasured each tournament, but couldn't look at the trophy until the fourth year for fear I'd sob and ruin the relaxed atmosphere for the others. But gradually the realization settled over me that someday it would be someone else's turn to be honored. I wanted that to happen before the person died. So, in 1988 I wrote to Morrie Driesenga, asking that the sixth tournament be the last one in Don's name. Undoubtedly, that would have happened eventually anyway, but giving them permission to change the direction of the tournament was a step deeper into resolution for me. I don't want to be one of those who discards all of the world's beauty by demanding eternal mourning from everyone.

One thing affecting resolution is how soon the survivor is able to grasp the reality of the death. Having seen Don die moved me faster toward resolution than would one whose husband was killed in war and buried overseas. Having an object—a body, a casket or a grave—helps us focus our grief and recognize the finality of our loss.

But that level often doesn't come without struggle over just how deeply God is involved in each life. I often remind myself—and others—that God never says, "Oops!" But does that mean He *planned* from the beginning of our marriage (in fact, from the beginning of our lives) that Don was to die at 39? Is He like some author who knows the story isn't interesting unless danger lurks, so He occasionally kills children or young parents? Or does He merely *know* the troubles that will descend upon our lives and wait for us to surrender the trauma— and ourselves—to Him so He can bring His good out of them?

I'm not comfortable with the thought of an almighty,

perfect God somehow being pulled around by my feeble struggles. Many areas of both my childhood and adult life have been so chaotic that I find peace, perhaps even sanity, in God's sovereign will. I *need* to know that He is ever present, encouraging and strengthening me as I try to follow His ways. Of course, defying either God's laws or those of nature (such as gravity) offer only intense consequences.

I best understand the will of God when I picture a house. Jesus stands at the front door, inviting us in. We can enter through the open door, climb in through the window, drop down the chimney or maybe—as I have often done—first chop a few holes in the roof. We can even refuse to enter the house at all, if we mistakenly believe grief is to be our permanent fate and thereby deny ourselves His healing touch. But it is only when we offer ourselves back to the One who gave Himself for us that we finally find peace—and the determination to go on with our life, stronger and ready to help others through their eventual suffering.

Note
1. Elisabeth Kübler-Ross, *On Death and Dying* (New York: Macmillan Publishing Co., 1970).

Chapter Three

Handling the Money

Before December 1982, I'd never balanced the checkbook or even read—let alone understood—the income tax papers Don asked me to sign. When his death catapulted me into financial decision- making, I was terrified my mistakes would rob Jay and Holly of the education we'd planned and force me into pushing a rusted shopping cart—piled with my books and quilts—through the streets of Detroit.

Don had wisecracked to friends he was worth more dead than alive, so, after his death, word got around that he had left me "very well off." To correct that assumption seemed disloyal, so I walked a scary, lonesome path as I learned to protect what I did have. I can think of at least 97 things I'd rather do than read about budgets and savings accounts, but I timidly began my journey by studying the financial-planning articles in the women's magazines. At least none of them would say, "I can't believe you have a master's degree and don't know this." Gradually I discovered the investment section in the local library.

Now I have three financial guides on my desk: *Answers to Your Family's Financial Questions* by Larry Burkett (Focus on the Family, 1987), *Faith and Savvy, Too!* by Judith Briles (Regal, 1988) and *Protecting Your Income and Your Family's Future* by William Brock Thoene (Bethany, 1989). But none of those were available in early 1983, and it took me a while to wade through the unfamiliar territory. Gradually though, I learned about pensions, mortgage equity and interest rates and even came up with the five money-management rules I later emphasized during the grief seminars:

1. Don't do anything without praying for guidance.
2. Don't make any major changes for the first year.
3. Get a good lawyer.
4. Get a good tax accountant.
5. Don't let the relatives borrow any money.

Pray for Guidance

Real security comes from the Lord—not from even the wisest of earthly investments. And even if we manage to gather great wealth, we are merely stewards of His property. I am well aware of the responsibilities I have for my children's care and I take 1 Timothy 5:8 (*NIV*) seriously: "If anyone does not provide for his relatives, and especially for his immediate family he has denied the faith and is worse than an unbeliever." But learning how to best provide for my children didn't happen overnight.

I've often said my B.A. and M.A. degrees are from Eastern Michigan University, but my "Ph.D." is from the School of Hard Knocks. Even before I became a widow, I'd already learned to pray about any major decision for three days. Financially, that translated into "If anybody's pressing for an immediate answer, run!"

I was amazed—and angered—by the number of stock-brokers and financial planners who contacted me within two weeks of Don's death—all offering to "help" me through the confusion. I'd already wisely deposited the check into certificates of deposit (CDs) at our bank and chose to have the money tied up for at least a year. That simple explanation cut short the caller's cajolery.

While my original motivation was fear, I could have chosen no better route. Not only did that relieve me of immediate worry (I do like to sleep at night) but it gave me time to study unfamiliar territory. As it turned out, the major investment I made was a down payment on our townhouse when the Lord called us to New York, but at least words such as "mutual funds" and "treasury bills" are no longer mysterious codes.

Some folks believe it's too "worldly" to be concerned about financial matters and even say money is evil. But 1 Timothy 6:10 says "the *love* of money is the root of all evil"—not money itself. Money is inanimate; how it's used is what matters.

Tithing is one way to make sure the money is put to good use. I realize the tithe is based on Old Testament practice rather than New Testament command, but I like giving to God's work. I can't go to northeastern Africa or the Bolivian jungles, but I can help others go. And I still get to be part of what God is doing for eternity.

Often I hear people say so many groups ask for money they don't know who to send it to. Here's an easy rule: Support only those missionaries or organizations you know or have studied. If you don't know the group well but feel as though the Lord is nudging you that way, do your homework. Ask other Christians what they know about the group, send for their annual report, call the Better Business Bureau to see if they have any complaints outstanding against them. If the organization is national or international in its ministry, contact the Evangelical Council for Financial Accountability and find out if the organization is a member in good standing. And as you're asking for the Lord's guidance, determine to follow it.

I often think of my friend—let's call her "Karen"—and her husband, "Jamie," who traded cars every time my friend turned around. When he brought home a second-hand yellow sedan they couldn't afford, Karen insisted they pray about the purchase for three days first. Jamie assented, but without Karen's knowledge verbally agreed to buy the car and had the dealership hold it for him. Less than three months later, the transmission went out, resulting in a massive repair bill. To Karen's credit, she didn't say, "I told you so," even as her husband guiltily confessed his past deception and present conviction the Lord would have spared them the hassle if only he had listened.

As you are asking for guidance, take comfort in the thought the Lord won't tell you anything in prayer that contradicts His Word, including urging you to grab a "get-rich-quick" scheme. Proverbs 21:5 (*NIV*) says, "The plans of the diligent lead to profit as surely as haste leads to poverty." Just a few chapters later, Proverbs 28:22 (*NIV*) says, "A stingy man is eager to get rich and is unaware that poverty awaits him."

One of the most popular "get- rich-quick" plans comes under the label of "commodities." Stay as far away from them as you possibly can. Sure, your third cousin's second husband may have made a fortune by dumping his wheat stock at the right time, but that same week countless others lost their life savings.

Being good stewards of God's money means that we

put it to good use—even if no more than allowing it to accumulate savings account interest—and not gamble with it. And any reputable stockbroker will tell you that one way of spelling "risk" is c-o-m-m-o-d-i-t-i-e-s.

If the thought of being a good steward for its own sake isn't persuasive enough, may I remind you that by taking care of the insurance money we not only keep from becoming a burden to our children but can, in fact, leave an inheritance. Proverbs 13:22 (*NIV*) says, "A good man leaves an inheritance for his children's children." And that goes for "a good woman" too.

Don't Make Any Major Changes for the First Year

Stress does awful things to even the most logical mind. But selling everything and running away—even under the guise of "a new beginning"—complicates the emotional healing. Knowing that Jay and Holly needed the stability only I could provide kept me from taking the next plane to Tahiti—or Kentucky. Even though the memory of their dad was in every corner of our home, being able to stay in familiar rooms helped us deal with our grief. During the next three years, the lack of previous upheaval helped them accumulate the emotional strength they'd need when we moved to New York.

The second good thing I did was keep our place at Maranatha Bible and Missionary Conference in Muskegon, Michigan. Within a month after Don's death, I received offers to sell but I was determined to hang on as long as I was financially able. Not only were most of our friends there but that was the only place Jay and Holly could remember being in the summer. When I had to sell it four years later, I had realized it wasn't the *place* itself I wanted—but Don and those lost years.

Because I remembered the way the illogical seems logical during that awful first year of grief, I've tried to caution others against making major decisions in those early months of trauma. Then in the summer of 1988, one of my cousins died from complications after giving birth to her fourth child. (Yes, that still happens today.)

Her husband gave us a new understanding of the term "wild with grief" as he announced he couldn't properly care for another baby and gave her up for adoption. Several women—including his own mother—offered to care for the child until he could work through his pain, but his mind was set. Besides, he said, it wasn't fair to the child to let this drag on. He insisted upon signing the legal papers and "getting on with his life."

I hate to be the one to tell you this, friend, but death is not *optional. If the Lord tarries,* all *of us are going to close our eyes here and open them in eternity.*

You know the rest of the story. Six months later, he was sitting in a lawyer's office, tearfully demanding help in getting his daughter back. But the state law was unforgiving and provided no loopholes despite his grief.

Get a Good Lawyer

Statistics tell us that between 65 to 80 percent of the population do not have a will. Some think they have plenty of time, some have gotten it into their heads they're going to live forever and still others are afraid they'll create a self-fulfilling prophecy. After all, if you have a will drawn up, you might need it!

I hate to be the one to tell you this, friend, but death is *not* optional. If the Lord tarries, *all* of us are going to close our eyes here and open them in eternity. And while we wait for Him, we are to "occupy" till He comes (see Luke 19:13).

Don and I had always had a handwritten will and even had it witnessed by friends. But Don had taught business law for years and knew the safest documents were the official ones. Within a week after his 1981 release from the hospital, he made a call to his school district, asking for their recommendations for an attorney who was a member "in good standing" of the American Bar Association. The appointment took less than an hour, but Don had done everything he could to make sure the property transfers would be done as effortlessly as possible—and without extensive delays. I'll always be grateful for his loving thoughtfulness.

Too many folks think, *Well, that's fine for people with property, but I don't own enough to go to all the trouble of doing a will.* Do you own more than the shirt on your back? Do you have a savings account? A checking account? Savings bonds? A gold watch that belonged to your father? If so, you want to have a say in how those things are distributed after your death.

And you can't assume that everything will automatically go to the spouse. Since laws vary from state to state, the worse assumption anyone can make is that the government will do things the way the individual had hoped. In many states, without a will stating otherwise, the wife receives only one-third to one-half of her husband's estate—even if her income purchased their property—

and the rest will go to the children. She will have to keep actual accounts of how she provides for the minors in her care and has no say in how they spend their portion of the money once they reach the legal age.

No will may mean the living expenses will force her to sell the family home, even if it was purchased with money from an earlier inheritance from her parents. And without a will, any distant relative can come swooping in with a claim against the estate, further tying up the proceedings.

Of course lawyers aren't cheap, but they can save us later money and hassle. And many of them devote their services in the evening for those who truly can't afford to have wills drawn up. A call to your local social services agency will let you know where that's available.

Part of the procedure requires that you provide your lawyer with a list of assets—naming your mortgage holder, insurance agent, bank account number, checking account number, pension holder and any investments you or your children have. If nothing else, the list will convince you that you have more assets than you thought.

One of the paragraphs in the will calls for the naming of an executor—or someone to take care of the financial details after the death. Choosing that person is harder than deciding who gets the savings account and the heirlooms. Who should that person be? A relative? Your lawyer?

Since every situation is different, I can't offer hard and fast rules. But I do suggest that you know the person well. Is he/she capable of handling details over several months? Notice, I'm not asking how much you love this person, just how well he/she is going to function under financial pressure. Will he/she give in to other family members who feel as though they were treated unfairly?

Wills should change as circumstances change. Once

Jay and Holly turn 18, I'll redo the document, giving them the right to chose where they want to live, including whether or not they want to sell this place. But for now, I've tried to anticipate all the problems they'll have if I die suddenly, including choosing guardians who have enough energy to guide them through the turbulent high school years. The ones who best fit that description are my close friends Carl and Marilyn Amann. Carl is a counselor now at the same high school where we taught English together all those years. Plus, they have a proven track record since their own six children are all serving the Lord in various capacities.

My situation is complicated because we're living in New York, but the children's designated guardians are in Michigan. Thus, I have two executors: my local lawyer—whom I accepted through the recommendation of dear friends—will handle the selling of our townhouse here, and transfer funds to the Michigan bank handling the details of Jay's and Holly's educations.

Obviously, I'm trusting that the Lord will allow me to see my children safely into their own families, but I've already learned that He doesn't always do things our way. By anticipating the things that *could* happen, I have freed myself from worry that a judge might appoint someone who would be not be a good choice for them.

Get a Good Tax Accountant

Don't let your brother-in-law handle your taxes unless he's a certified public accountant (CPA) and has always done them for you. Widows are especially vulnerable because most of our husbands handled the financial decisions. Our fears make us only too eager to turn financial responsibility over to someone else again. Don't do it. Even as you ask for counsel, do your own homework and learn all you can about the decisions only you should be making. And keep praying.

After Don's death, our lawyer asked who did our tax preparation. When I answered, "Don," he recommended the accountants who handled his business records and insisted I make an immediate appointment.

In that first call to the CPA, I heard words I only vaguely remembered Don using—"tax liability," "deductions," "adjusted gross income." Then he asked that I bring copies of our tax returns for the past five years to his office.

Copies of tax returns? Where on earth would Don have put those? I looked in all the usual places, including his filing cabinet that I had taken over for my writing assignments. Nothing. Next I looked in all of the illogical places, finally cleaning out every drawer in our bedroom. Still nothing.

After three hours of searching every drawer on both floors, I could think of nothing else to do except call my "big brother," Carl Amann.

"How do I get copies from the IRS?" I asked. "Don must have thrown ours out. You know how he hated clutter."

Carl chuckled. "Ah, come on. He was a business teacher. There's no way he's thrown those out. They're in that house someplace. If you don't find them soon, Marilyn and I'll come over and help you look."

After I hung up the phone, I remained seated, leaning my head against the spot where my beloved Scot had rested his. "Donnie, *where* are those papers?" I waited for his laughing retort, but only the January wind answered.

"Donnie, you always handled the taxes. Where are those copies?" Silence.

How was I going to survive if I couldn't even find five lousy tax returns? I leaned forward, my hands covering my face. "Lord, you've promised to supply all my needs. Well, I need those tax papers and I've looked everywhere. Please tell me where they are."

Even before I could say "Amen," the image of a brown briefcase sitting under the basement steps came to mind. We'd moved the filing cabinet up to my office on the second floor several months ago but hadn't gotten around to taking all of the files. I bounded down the steps and grabbed the briefcase. Of course, it was filled with tax papers.

As I counted out the needed copies, I thought of my having asked Don just a few minutes before to tell me where they were. I'd been talking to the wrong person. It wasn't until I'd prayed and asked for the Lord's help that I remembered the briefcase.

I quickly gathered the copies for 1976-81 but still searched through all of the papers, looking for—what? Perhaps a letter from Don to encourage me. How I would have loved to have found a note in his bold handwriting, saying, "You *can* do this, San." But nothing but tax papers were in the case. I was still very much on my own.

Don had kept only the essential records each tax year, but I was terrified someone official would demand to see every receipt. Thus, for the first few years, I kept everything—even labeling a box "Important papers that I don't know what to do with." Now I've culled out the unnecessary and made room for the rest.

Along the way, I've learned I don't have to keep cancelled checks nor tax returns more than six years old, receipts for items I no longer own, bank statements more than a year old, monthly missions receipts (I need only the annual receipt) nor receipts more than six months old for utilities. Not keeping everything eliminates massive clutter.

A couple of months ago, I was in one of those classic cleaning moods and discovered a cardboard box full of cancelled checks from the late '60s—when we were still newlyweds. It took me several evenings to sort through more than 20 years of checks, but I wanted to keep the ones marking milestones—for our first home, for graduate courses, for Jay's and Holly's deliveries. Letting go is never easy for me, so, of course, all those checks in Don's handwriting triggered countless memories. But keeping those pieces of paper hadn't brought him back, and I finally tossed most of the checks into the garbage without another thought.

Don't Let the Relatives Borrow Money

You are not a bank—even though your extended family may treat you like one. That's another advantage to putting the insurance check immediately into certificates of deposit; you can't get at the money after hearing all those sad stories. If you ignore the first part of this rule—"Don't let the relatives borrow money"— please listen to the second part—"But if you do, make sure you have them sign a note."

Karen's sister and her husband had struggled financially since the beginning of their marriage, caught into thinking they could buy everything they wanted now and just pay it off gradually while they enjoyed it. By the time Karen received the settlement from her husband's estate, her sister, husband and two children were living in his mother's unfinished basement, unable to handle rising rents along with their credit card balances.

When they found a small house they could afford, they didn't have the money for a down payment. Would Karen help them get their children out of the basement? Of course.

Several months later, as Karen met with the accountant preparing her income tax return, this information came out. The accountant was adamant that she get a signed note. Karen was hurt. "But she's my sister."

> *If you ignore the first part of this rule—"Don't let the relatives borrow money"— please listen to the second part—"But if you do, make sure you have them sign a note."*

"I don't care," he retorted. "You get that note. Tell them I insisted you have to have it for income tax purposes. Tell them I yelled at you. Just get it."

Reluctantly Karen did exactly that, apologizing all the while. A year later, she was thanking the accountant for his foresight—her sister and husband were in the process of an ugly divorce, and that signed note was pivotal in his releasing his rights to the house. He said if his ex-wife would pay off the note, he'd sign off on the house and she wouldn't have to sell it. Their two children could remain in their home instead of living in someone else's basement.

Perhaps you won't be asked for thousands of dollars, but just for a "few hundred." Giving adult children money out of a misplaced sense of responsibility or even out of guilt does them no favors, nor are you denying your faith (see 1 Tim. 5:8). Sometimes we best provide for our families by saying no. But if you do decide you'd rather let them have the money than worry about not letting them have it, chalk it up mentally to a gift. If you decide you'll never see the money again, at least you won't be disappointed when they don't repay you.

If you think I'm being harsh, let me end with an all-too-familiar true story. One of my friends out West lives in a senior citizens' complex. Each year their neighborhood gains another three or four new widows, most of whom are bewildered by the financial decisions swooping upon them. One widow, decided she'd solve her problems by putting her house and her money in her son's name, thereby relieving her of any decision-making.

Poor choice. The son got into a financial bind and sold her home! As of this writing, his mother doesn't have an idea of where she's going to live or what she'll do for the rest of her life. And all because she was afraid of learning to manage her own money.

Because I am God's child, He is concerned about every aspect of my life. I like the three verbs in Luke 11:9 (*NIV*): "Ask and it will be given to you; seek and you will find; knock and the door will be opened to you." Asking, seeking and knocking are words of *our* action. Even as much as we long to be rescued from problems, we still are responsible for the results. The Lord has promised to help us, but we have to take that first step.

CHAPTER FOUR

How to Help

Perhaps you aren't the one grieving, but want to help someone who is. You have several things you can do to help your friends grieve appropriately.

Encourage the Griever to Talk

People who care about others want to *say* something that will ease the pain, but it's more important to hurt with them.

The most important thing you can do is listen. Listen while she describes the squealing brakes and the sight of her 6-year-old lying face down in the street. The easy thing is to say, "No, that's OK. I don't need the details." But she needs to give them, painful though they are.

For the ones who haven't seen the accident site, they may need to look at the marks the careening car left on the telephone pole. Such curiosity isn't morbid—it's normal. And it deserves attention.

Identify the Source of Pain

As a friend listens to the griever, he often hears what the person is really saying. The two most common emotions are anger and guilt—and they're often tangled together.

Dr. Canine listened to a widow rant against the hospital for sending her husband home when his brain tumor wasn't responding to chemotherapy.

"They should have kept him there," she said. "He was too sick to be home. He was so confused he couldn't find the bathroom and went in our bedroom instead. Those stupid doctors!"

As Dr. Canine asked questions, he learned the man had died a few days after the incident. The woman was actually angry at *herself* for having yelled at her confused husband. When John identified the source of her anger, she sobbed. Once she faced the anger, she could allow the healing to begin.

Help Sort Out Feelings

We feel better when we can express our feelings. If it's a glorious morning, somehow verbalizing that thought makes the day even better. And if we can verbalize the painful feelings, the pain is lessened. This is where a good listener can make a big difference. Without sounding clinical, we can say, "How are you doing—really? Feel like talking?"

Denial and avoidance are two common reactions in our society to loss. Denial is the this-isn't-happening-to-me feeling. Avoidance is the "OK, it happened. Now I'm going to forget about it." Both mean later problems, unless they are identified and resolved. Identifying the emotion often provides the needed release.

Often anger seeps through the words. Perhaps it's directed toward the rotten weather that made the roads slippery that day, the policeman who responded to the call, God for letting the person die or even the deceased himself. All that is normal. The griever needs to hear that it's OK to be angry—even at the deceased or God. Notice that I didn't say "desirable," but "OK."

Many people are uncomfortable with the thought that it's OK to be angry at God . . . . God is so real to me that I dare to gripe at Him when my life is turned inside out.

When Bev died in an accident, Carl was left with three children, all under the age of three. Into his grief crept a subtle anger. As soon as he identified it, he expressed it aloud: "Yeah, Bev, you're in heaven enjoying yourself, and I'm still here trying to raise three children!" That simple statement not only allowed him to zero in on what he was feeling, but it also helped him direct it appropriately instead of lashing out at the people—or children—around him.

Many people are uncomfortable with the thought that it's OK to be angry at God. They mouth all the right words about God's comfort, but deep down they wonder: If He's so good, how come He didn't stop the tragedy? I decided long ago that God can handle our anger. He knows our hearts and sees the anger anyway, so why shouldn't we talk to Him about it?

God is so real to me that I dare to gripe at Him when my life is turned inside out. Oh, I *want* to be one of those placid saints who never complain and immediately accept everything as coming from His hand and, therefore, wonderful. But even the Presbyterian in me has a long way to go before I can watch a young life dissolve before my eyes and then say, "Hey, that's neat, God. Thanks!" Yet I have learned that He will bring His good out of whatever we give to Him. And He will comfort us in tangible and profound ways—if we'll let Him.

The anger that's a normal part of every grief can be constructive or destructive. Constructive anger forms support groups—such as Friends and Families, a group for those who've lost through murder—or educational groups such as Mothers Against Drunk Driving. Destructive anger lashes out at everyone around us or turns inward in the form of depression or illness—as I learned when I was angry about Uncle Lawrence's untimely death. It's not uncommon for that anger to be misdirected toward doctors, police, even funeral directors.

When Don died, one of his relatives was so angry that he repeatedly sniped about the work the funeral home had done. I was the one who had sat by Don's hospital bed during those last days and witnessed incredible deterioration in his condition, so I was relieved to see the mortician's skill. But the relative insisted they add more cosmetic cover to the small lump above the forehead where the chemotherapy shunt had been placed just under the skin.

At the time, I couldn't talk to the relative about what was happening as I barely had enough energy to get through the day myself. Instead I apologized to the director for the rudeness. He looked surprised; anger was such a typical reaction from family members that he hadn't noticed. Then he said, "Believe me, that's nothing."

Two years later, when I was working there as the Community Service Director, I understood his forgiveness. Some families carried such intense anger that the director had to insist they appoint a representative to speak for all of them. Others boiled with such anger toward each other that the staff constantly circulated, talking to those needing special attention.

> *God knew what He was doing when He gave us tear ducts. They are our release valves . . . . It's better if the tears can flow now so we can move on later.*

When I'd give the grief presentations before doctors' groups—in order to build even stronger relations between the hospitals and funeral homes—I could always get their attention by remarking that the patient's survivors who have unresolved anger are more apt to file a malpractice suit.

Unexpressed anger can be equally harmful.

My friend Deborah Staton tells about her then nine-year-old son, Shane, screaming as he charged into the house. With his left hand, he was clutching the right—and blood was oozing between his fingers.

"Shane! What happened? Let me see it."

"No! You'll hurt me!"

"Shane, Mommy can't help unless you show me your hand."

"No! Get away!"

Finally, Debi had to wrestle him down to see the injury. As she carefully opened his fingers, she was expecting to see tendon and bone, but it was only one of those top-layer-off skin scrapes that bleed a lot. After washing and dressing the wound, Debi released Shane to return to his ball game.

As she was putting away the first aid kit and marveling at his dramatics, Debi was suddenly struck with the thought she'd been doing the same thing to God. A recent disappointment had so hurt her she couldn't even pray about it. It was as though God was saying, "Let me see your hurt," while Debi stood with fists clenched, saying, "I'm *not* angry!"

Don't Condemn Emotions

Romans 12:15 is perfect for those who want to help the griever: "Rejoice with them that do rejoice, and weep with them that weep." It's important that the griever have freedom to express the needed emotions—tears, of course, but even laughter. It's unfortunate when others think everyone should grieve at the same pace. Thus, if they see the widow laughing, they think, "Boy, it certainly didn't take her long to get over that." She's not over her grief, she's merely enjoying the momentary joke.

Our first weeks at Maranatha after Don's death were made easier by special friends who supported rather than judged my moods. Often when I cried, they cried with me. And if I needed to laugh, they rejoiced. Their acceptance of whatever emotion I displayed helped move me that much closer to healing.

The first Sunday after the funeral is especially hard for many people, especially if they were together in church the previous week. In one short week, the person has died, the funeral has taken place and everything has changed. My first Sunday back, Jay and Holly were in their classes, so I entered the large sanctuary all by myself.

The usher asked, "Just one?"

I nodded. "Unfortunately just one."

I sat in my usual spot directly in front of the pulpit. As

Dr. Hess preached, I missed Don's nudges. Then I missed hearing his tenor voice reaching the high notes during the closing hymn. But I was there every Sunday and listened with tears running down my cheeks. Finally one early September morning, I knew my healing had begun when, at the end of the sermon, I finally smiled at Dr. Hess.

Once I apologized to him for crying so much. His reply was gentle. "The important thing is you kept coming, kept being open to the message and what God had for you."

I often ask, "Is God in charge or not?" As a good Presbyterian, I know He is. And it's OK to proclaim His sovereignty with tears running down our cheeks. He understands our pain and will help us—if we allow Him to.

Shortly before we moved to New York, one of the women in the Bible study said to me, "Oh, you had the most marvelous testimony after your husband died. You never cried; you were just a pillar of strength."

I was astounded, then irritated. "No, you just never *saw* me cry. I'm sorry if that 'weakens' my testimony, but remember, even Jesus cried."

Undoubtedly, I disappointed her, but spiritual games are something I refuse to play now. Someday she too will lose someone she loves. If I had lied to her, allowing her to believe that "good" Christians don't cry even in the worst sorrow, then I would have been doing her a disservice by heaping guilt upon her future tears. Or worse yet, perhaps she wouldn't have given herself permission to cry and would have held all of that pain inside. We are truly "fearfully and wonderfully made" (Ps. 139:14) and are constructed in such a way that we must grieve.

God knew what He was doing when He gave us tear ducts. They are our release valves. Several years ago, *The Detroit Free Press* reported a scientific study analyzing the content of tears. A group of folks peeled onions for the researchers. The resulting tears consisted of salt and water.

Then those same people were shown sad movies. As the viewers cried, the researchers collected more tears. This time the drops contained the usual salt and water— and a toxic chemical. But haven't we always known that? Think of the times we've responded to "What's wrong?" with "Nothing. I just need a good cry."

If we're not allowed to cry, either because of our own or society's standards, the toxins stay in the brain, producing other problems. It's better if the tears can flow now so we can move on later. That's why the ones who were my greatest comfort simply put their arms around me and cried too.

Avoid Hoof-in-Mouth Comforting

No one quoting Romans 8:28 offered comfort. In fact, I felt as though they had come to do their good Christian duty. When they walked out the door, they may have felt better, but I certainly didn't.

Let me stress I do believe Romans 8:28. "And we know that all things work together for good to them that love God, to them who are the called according to his purpose." But I need to quote it to myself, not hear it from someone else.

Know what amazed me? The women who said they knew just how I felt as they stood there with their husbands! But the prize for the worst "comfort" comes from a letter to Ann Landers: A friend visited the parents of the nine-year-old son who had been tragically killed. "I know just how you feel," she said. "Our dog died a month ago and we're still grieving." Remember, Job's friends sat with him for seven days and never got into trouble until they opened their mouths.

Honor Those Promises

Another way to help someone move through grief is by fulfilling promises. A favorite parting at the funeral home is "Call me if you need anything." But two months pass and everyone has gotten on with life—except the widow. Suddenly she realizes the car needs tires but doesn't know where to get new ones. She'll be able to move back into life faster if she gets help from the first person she calls. Being put off or hearing too soon "You've got to learn to make these decisions yourself" turn her away from grieving for an individual and into grieving for the way her life has turned out.

Offer Practical Help

Suddenly having to do the things the spouse used to do can be overwhelming. I'll never forget answering the door the day after Don's funeral and finding Nancy Harrison there. Timidly she said, "I've come to help you clean your house, if you'll let me. I didn't call because I knew you'd say everything was fine."

Not only did Nancy offer to meet a *specific* need, but she stepped through my emotional wall and risked rejection in order to help. I wisely let her in and we worked together all morning, rapidly deepening our sound friendship.

I advise caution here though because not everyone has the same needs. The needs will vary especially if the wife is the one who died. Some widowers need help in normal household tasks since the laundry, cooking and even grocery shopping may overwhelm them. Others may have been the principal cooks for years but are suddenly bewildered by the checkbook. The most important thing we can do is ask what areas they need help in.

The expression, "Women grieve; men replace," came out of the statistics of the rapid remarriage of widowers. I witnessed that fact in the seminars for families who had lost members during the previous year: The widows brought Kleenex, the widowers brought a girlfriend or new wife.

Several years ago, *Time* magazine analyzed why widowers remarry so soon. They considered differences in physical and emotional characteristics and societal conditioning, but no firm conclusions were drawn. The following week a woman sent the editor what I hope was a tongue-in-cheek answer: "When a man loses his wife, his work doubles. When a woman loses her husband, her work is cut in half."

Of course that may be an amusing overgeneralization, but some people have trouble quickly absorbing tasks they've never had to do. Many older women don't know how to fill the car's fuel tank. One deacon routinely asks new widows, "Do you know how to pump gas?" It's amazing the number of women, even in this modern day, who don't know how.

I was one of those women. I drove for the first 15 years of our marriage but had never filled the tank. When Don's illness forced me to learn, I was frightened.

Imagine my surprise when I learned it's a simple five-step plan—(1) take the nozzle off the side of the pump, (2) flip the switch up, (3) unscrew the gas cap on my car, (4) insert the nozzle and (5) squeeze the handle. The scary mystery dissolved. That evening, I teased Don, saying he'd always insisted upon pumping the gas because he didn't want me to know how easy it really was. I'm sure he would be surprised to know that I've since learned how to change the oil—including both filters, too.

The biggest problem for the person wanting to assist the living is: When is it time to quit? For the middle-aged daughter whose bed-ridden mother has died, you may be needed just during that busy funeral week. For the widow with young children, you may be needed to provide an emotional harbor for several weeks—until she gets used to being on her own.

Sometimes the griever has to help set those limits. The week after Don's funeral, Cathy Fife sent over a lasagne dinner. I still wasn't up to cooking for just the three of us, so her offering was especially welcome. The next week, her chicken divan appeared on our table.

Each time I had expressed my sincere appreciation, thinking that was the end of it. When she was still sending food over the fourth week, I knew she needed permission to stop cooking for us. I called her and tactfully let her know it was OK to stop. She sounded relieved by my call.

Often it works well for the giver to set a time limit: "For the next three weeks, I'd like to bring dinner over on Thursday nights."

Don't Expect Instant Healing

It amazes me how quickly our society expects us who are bereaved to get our lives back into balance. If we were baseball players and had accidents that resulted in the loss of our legs, no one would expect us to be back out on the diamond the next month. Losing someone—either to death or divorce—is an amputation. A special person and the life we shared are gone forever. We can't immediately jump back into the mainstream of living. Rebuilding our lives takes time.

The greatest problems come when the one grieving doesn't allow himself time to work through all of the sorrow. Occasionally Dr. Canine is asked if he thinks it's too early for someone to start dating again. He always refers the questioner to the "Three Cs"—Companionship, Common Interests and Commitment—as a personal measuring stick.

People need one another, so dating fills the need of someone to talk to. But all too often folks jump from companionship to commitment, skipping the important middle step of common interests. Then two months after the wedding—if that long—as though awakening from a deep sleep, a man discovers his first wife is dead and some stranger is sitting in her place at the table. The grief becomes complicated rapidly.

Often a griever is startled when she finds herself attracted to someone else—especially if it's someone for whom such feelings aren't appropriate—her pastor or a married friend. That's such a common occurrence it even has a name: transference. All the energy and attention that had gone into the marriage has to go somewhere, so it's directed toward a friend or special co-worker.

Misunderstood transference can tempt lonely people into making inappropriate commitments or even committing adultery. Too often we hear of a pastor who was counseling a distraught woman and then had an affair with her, destroying his marriage and ministry. What the pair had accepted as love was actually transference. Recognizing it—and waiting it out—would have spared both much pain.

And while we're on the subject, let's talk about what the widowed spouse is to do about sexual desires. Different authors have different ideas but most agree that the only thing that really helps is refocusing that energy into work or creative projects. I first heard about this concept in my college literature class as the professor lectured about the great artists whose sublimated sexual urges resulted in greater creative energy. Newly married, my first thought was *No way!* But since Don's death, I've written numerous articles, several video presentations and three more books. I guess the professor was right.

Help Define Normal Behavior

The grief process often includes behavior and thought patterns so different from what the griever is used to that she may think she's losing her mind. It helps to have somebody say, "No, you're not crazy; you're grieving. This will pass."

Often this comes through temporary memory lapses. Bill commented that after his wife died, he found himself in a bar without remembering how he had gotten there. Normally only a social drinker, he was rightly concerned about this new behavior. Talking it through and making a conscious effort to reach for the phone—instead of the car keys—and calling a friend got him over the roughest time.

One of my favorite secular sayings is "Untried virtue is no virtue." How many times have we heard, "I'd never do that"? But unless we've experienced the same tragedy, we don't know what we'd do. How much better to say, "I *hope* I'd never do that."

In the first three years after Don's death, I traveled to six foreign countries. In every place, I caught myself seriously scanning the crowds, looking for Don. Intellectually, I knew he was dead—I'd seen him die—but emotionally I kept expecting him to appear at my elbow with his, "Ah, San! What kept you?" Since I know even normal minds create such fantasies, I continued the daily routine without undue concern. If I hadn't known such goofy thoughts are normal, I might have huddled in a corner, waiting for an ambulance and straitjackets.

This is where a trusted friend, especially one who's been through similar grief, is invaluable. If the griever knows she is safe and can express whatever is on her mind, she'll work through the strange thought patterns much more quickly.

Accept Individual Differences

Different people react to grief in different ways. Some go through boxes of tissues through the roughest parts of grieving. Others choke up, their eyes filling with tears that never fall. The problem comes when criers and noncriers judge the other's reaction to grief. I'm a crier, but at Don's funeral I concentrated upon just getting through the ordeal. I knew if I started crying, I'd never be able to get through the service and the 36-mile drive to Chelsea for the burial. Later, I made up for those dry eyes.

The following Memorial Day, I saw another facet of individual differences in grief. The first time the three of us went back to Maranatha Bible Conference, I wasn't sure I could face opening our mobile home alone. As I pulled in, six of the Maranatha young men who had been especially close to Don were hurriedly raking the leaves, trying to finish before I arrived. That was their way of saying, "We loved him."

Within a few minutes, other Maranatha family members arrived. Morrie Driesenga gave me his fatherly hug and cried with me. Later Bob Jelsema gestured toward the faucet under my mobile home and said, "Let's get the water turned on."

Emotional support. Practical help. Both were expressions from two very different men—yet both expressed love and both were exactly what I needed at the moment.

Be There

This is a scary idea for many because they think the griever's needs are limitless. But *continued* support doesn't mean *endless* support.

The greatest complaint many of us have is: Where are all the people who said, "Call me anytime"?

I remember thinking, *What they actually mean is "Call me anytime—as long as it's not too late, not during dinner or my favorite TV show, and not too often—and only in the first two weeks."*

Grievers are caught in a time warp: each moment rolls toward us, slowly, heavily, a reminder that our life has been changed forever. But like it or not, life goes on. The problems come when our friends expect us to move through our grief at the same rate they have moved through theirs.

In the beginning of my grief, one area remained especially painful: Friday nights. Don and I had gone out to dinner—often just pizza—almost every weekend for 16 years. How I looked forward to those times when we could verbally share our week and solidify our commitment to each other.

But after he died, Friday nights were monsters to slink past. How nice it would have been if some of our close friends—who knew our routine—had included me for an occasional Friday night out. For the first few months, I didn't have the energy to venture out anyway, so it didn't matter that Jay, Holly and I ordered pizza, watched unamusing situation-comedies and went to bed by 9:00 P.M.

But finally, I decided I'd have to grab the bull by the

horns. I invited couples to join me on Friday nights. My insecurity wouldn't allow me to believe they'd want to spend the evening eating pizza with *me,* so I asked them to be my guests at expensive restaurants. Of course, that merely compounded my loneliness.

An easier way of offering continued support is by remembering important dates. Again, the hesitancy is "But I don't want to remind them." Believe me, you're not.

In Ethiopia—before the ravishing famines—40 days of mourning were customary. During that time, the grieving family rested, received visitors and ate high protein grains. On the forty-first day, they limped back into life, knowing their friends would again send special greetings on the eightieth day. The first anniversary was marked by a special church service. For the next six years, the family had the option of a quiet service, taking the grain to the church and receiving personal blessings from the priests or sending the grain with the understanding the priests would pray for the family.

Keeping track of various death anniversaries, of course, was complicated, so most families had a separate book to record the dates. In our outwardly stoic, three-days-and-get-on-with-life society, it's easy to dismiss the more involved grieving of another culture as morbid. But I really think the Ethiopians understand the *need* for grieving more than we do. And I'm convinced they also understand the human body's stress level better.

After Don died, paperwork that could be delayed I dumped onto my writing desk until the cluttered area became a burden. But I didn't have the physical energy to deal with it. Weeks passed until I had to tackle that desk just so it wouldn't torment me. I sorted, tossed, filed or answered every piece of paper until the desk was clear. As

I admired the restored order, I picked up the calendar, wondering what day it was. It was the forty-first day.

Another way for friends to offer emotional support is by remembering anniversaries and birthdays. Jotting down the date when the person comments, "The fifteenth of next month, we would have been married 26 years" and following up with a card or a call—or an invitation to dinner—continues the healing.

Don died less than two months before our seventeenth wedding anniversary, so the first February 5—a Saturday—loomed before me like some ancient trap door. Rose Keilhacker, invited the three of us to their club for swimming and lunch—and conversation. With her help, I got through the day.

Anniversaries 18 and 19 were less traumatic because I was adjusting to widowhood. But a few weeks before the milestone of the twentieth, I wrote numerous friends and asked them to pray for me since that was the day Don had promised to ask me to marry him. Several years earlier I realized we'd been married 12 years—without my ever having been *asked.* Don had *told* me we were getting married.

When I shared my revelation, he grinned and said, "Well, maybe one of these days I'll ask you."

"Don! I'm serious about this. We've been married all these years and have two children. I want to be asked."

Undoubtedly he wanted to get back to the televised game. "Ooookay. Tell you what. I will—for our twentieth wedding anniversary."

He may have thought that was the end of the discussion, but I hugged thoughts of that coming milestone. Maybe we'd finally go to Scotland. We'd visit his cousins near Bathgate, touch the walls of the ancestral home, walk along the moors. He'd pick a bouquet of heather and ask me to marry him—or at least say he was glad I had married him. In reality, Don would have golfed at St. Andrew's while I walked along the moor with his cousin Jean Harris, but the hopeless romantic in me found comfort.

Unfortunately, reality and our dreams seldom blend. And even though my widowhood had taught me that, I still dreaded the steady approach of February 5, 1986. Asking for help is difficult for me, but alerting several close friends to the importance of the day was the best thing I could have done. Not only did the sharing of my emotional stress actually lessen it, but I was surrounded by prayer. Many friends sent notes to encourage me, and Tedd and Ruth Bryson even added an unexpected bouquet of flowers. The emotional support helped me move on.

Know When to Quit

No matter how well intentioned we are, we will run into situations where nothing we do helps. When those times come, we need to refer the individuals to counselors who *can* help. But this is only for those stuck in one stage. If the griever is still crying after two months, don't suggest counseling—invite her for coffee and a chat. But if she hasn't combed her hair or brushed her teeth during those two months, then you might ask if she'd like to talk to someone who can help her. Again, don't overreact.

A few years ago, Dr. Canine received a call from an adult daughter reporting her father's lack of progress and asking, "Will you see him *now*?" Months before, her mother had come home from Christmas shopping, draped her coat over the back of the chair and toppled over with a massive heart attack.

In the days following her death, her husband refused to let anyone touch that coat. At two months, the family starting calling Dr. Canine. "It's been two months, you've got to do something."

He asked what other troubling things the man was doing. Nothing. He had returned to work and was still attending church. The only problem was the coat. Dr. Canine suggested they ignore it. But they still called every month to report that the coat was still there. And every month he suggested they ignore it.

That went on for almost nine months. Finally one August afternoon, the father picked up the coat, handed it to his daughter and said, "Find somebody who'll need this." When he was ready to let go, he did.

At one of my seminars, a woman asked how she could help her friend Mary who insisted upon signing her deceased husband's name to greeting cards even though he had died five years earlier. The action was giving her friends the creeps. When they asked her why she continued to do that, she replied that she didn't want their friends to forget him. And, undoubtedly, she was concerned she'd forget him too.

I suggested she try signing only her name but adding a note such as "If Fred were here, he'd add his good wishes too." That compromise finally allowed her to let go of her grief and move on with her life. But it wouldn't have happened if her friend hadn't cared enough to help.

CHAPTER FIVE

Abnormal Grief

Within our study of normal emotions and activities, perhaps we ought to take a few moments to look at some abnormal ones. Four major categories are in this area.

Chronic

The grieving here is constant and overwhelming—and has gone on for weeks. If young children are in the family, the survivor hasn't been able to take over their care yet. If she's older, perhaps she still can't get dressed, brush her teeth or comb her hair without someone directing her every move. "No, Ma. Your arm goes here."

If this behavior happens within the first couple of weeks, it's OK and is still part of the initial stage in which everything seems to move in slow motion. She may even feel that her helper's voice is coming from the end of a long tunnel. All that's normal. But if it's gone on for weeks, then it's time for direct action.

For the most part, that intervention comes in the form

of other survivors taking the newest one by the hand and showing her it is possible to go on. Sometimes all it takes is another widow staying with her for a few days and occasionally saying, "Now come on. It's time to get dressed."

While most people move through even this intense stage eventually, it still may take professional intervention via a knowledgeable grief therapist. Usually though, it comes through some sudden realization. Some of the widows I talked to mentioned seeming to awaken from a bad dream, realizing their children had gone to school that morning, but not knowing who had gotten breakfast for them. Concern for the children is often the triggering factor.

When my Grandpa Ted Picklesimer was only 22, he died after his right leg was crushed by a coal-mining car. His children were ages four years (Aunt Reva), two years (Dad) and six weeks (Uncle Ishmael). After the funeral, my Grandma Katie took to her bed—as they say in the South. She literally collapsed and had no strength to move or to care for her children.

The women in that little mountain holler (valley) took turns caring for the children, but she was so despondent they thought they'd soon bury her. They'd seen that happen before.

One morning her father, Big John T. Dunn, burst into her bedroom. "Katie, if you die too, who's gonna take care of these youngins?"

Her eyes opened wide. Immediately she swung her feet onto the floor and took the baby from the hovering neighbor. Her father left as quickly as he had arrived; his daughter was going to be just fine. Not only did she rebuild her life, but years later Katie Dunn Picklesimer Lovely would be my example when my own widowhood seemed overpowering.

Delayed

This is the most common abnormal grief response. The manifestation of this response is usually calm, even magnificent acceptance of the tragedy. At the funeral home, she quotes the right Scriptures and actually comforts those who came to comfort her. But months later, when everyone else has gotten on with their lives, she falls apart. She may become a real pain, picking fights with everyone over the least thing, demanding her way in inappropriate areas. Or she may become so deeply depressed she can't function.

This type of abnormality also shows up when the grief has been postponed, as, for example, until after a court settlement. Grief therapists all have stories of parents who went through a court battle after the death of a child. The battle may drag on for three years, with the parents concentrating upon the procedure. Once the case is settled however, the grief is allowed to surface and is as intense as if the child had died three hours earlier instead of three years ago.

The grief also may be delayed if the death occurred during the survivor's childhood and she wasn't allowed then to grieve. One of my friends was five when her parents were killed in an accident. Her grandmother, who never showed her own grief, didn't allow the little girl to go to the funeral, saying it was no place for children.

For all of the years "Teri" lived with her grandmother, her parents were never again mentioned. On the surface, she had adjusted well. But when she married, she panicked so profoundly each time her husband had to be away on business she sought professional help.

When the therapist asked about her parents, Teri sobbed throughout the session, remembering that frightened five-year-old who didn't understand what had happened. Her assignment that week was to talk to two ancient aunts and find out the details. Once she was allowed to grieve, she could finally move on with the rest of her life—without the obsession that her husband was going to leave her too.

This delayed grief can also surface years later after a miscarriage or an abortion. Each time I presented this area at a retreat, I'd meet more than a few women who were still suffering over a child they had lost years before. Many of them were part of the 1970s copper IUD users who had been advised to have therapeutic abortions to prevent the onset of septic poisoning that already had taken a dozen lives. One young mother of two had died only 11 hours after the sudden appearance of the fever. After that incident, numerous doctors discarded their "wait and see" attitudes and insisted upon abortions for all those with dislodged IUDs.

In October 1986, after I had spoken at a Winning Women retreat in Grand Rapids, Michigan, a lady in her midforties timidly approached. She had had such an abortion 10 years earlier but no one in her family, other than her husband, knew. Every June, the memories flooded in until she finally decided to talk to her doctor about it. His response was less than sympathetic: "If you can't handle it, get counseling." She stood before me, twisting a piece of tissue. "All I wanted to do was talk to him about it. . . ."

Even though the medical profession had said she didn't have a choice, she still felt if she'd trusted the Lord more, she wouldn't have submitted to the abortion. Her shoulders were slumped in defeat. She knew the medical reasons for the abortion, but she had a deeper need.

I got right to the point: "Have you asked the Lord's forgiveness?"

She nodded.

"Have you forgiven yourself?"

Tears sprang to her eyes. "No. How can I forgive myself for killing my baby?"

I put my arms around her. "First John 1:9 (*NIV*) says, 'If we confess our sins, he is faithful and just and will forgive us our sins and purify us from all unrighteousness.' Please accept His forgiveness by forgiving yourself."

Often the survivor doesn't want to talk about the person who has died. . . . It may take gentle questions about his family member or friend to help him sort through the details of his specific grief.

By that time, she was sobbing against my shoulder, so I put my arms around her and prayed quietly, asking that in the days ahead the Lord would remind her of His forgiveness so she could accept healing. At my "Amen," she gave me a solid hug and hurried to meet her friends. I noticed that her shoulders weren't as slumped as they'd been before.

Since then I've often thought of her and prayed that the Lord will guide her as she shares the dark secret she's carried all those years. I trust she is free from her burden, but I've seen too many times where people hold another's testimony against her. The Lord's forgiveness is pure—and our confessed sins are not only forgiven but forgotten.

But other Christians don't always have that attitude and base future leadership positions upon past, forgiven sins. "But my dear, do we really want HER on our right-to-life committee? After all, she did have an abortion herself. Oh, you didn't know?"

Exaggerated

Often the survivor doesn't want to talk about the person who has died but becomes obsessed with the subject of death and dying. He may collect Victorian funeral jewelry, read books on world funeral customs or take classes on death and dying, supposedly to help others who are hurting. Certainly some of this is normal curiosity and honest attempts at easing the pain of others. But if he prefers to talk about the world's loss rather than his personal one, it may take gentle questions about his family member or friend to help him sort through the details of his specific grief.

I remember one widow's group where most of the women started passing the tissue box as soon as I introduced myself. My plan for the evening was to direct their thinking into ways they could use personal hurt to help others. They also could share some of the ways they had learned from their pain. One gal insisted she was in the group just to give her someplace to go each month. She kept concentrating upon the grief of the others but refused to say anything about her own loss.

After the meeting, she asked what were the possibilities she could work for our funeral home. "Dead people just fascinate me," she said. I didn't encourage her to apply.

Masked

This response is similar to our society's custom of avoidance and denial. In this, the personhood of the survivor isn't strong enough to cope with his loss, so he must mask over his pain in order to continue living. One of my friends returned from his wife's funeral and insisted his adult children get rid of her jewelry and clothing within the hour. They were astonished. They were just barely coping with their own grief; how could he be so strong?

Inappropriate responses can result in greater problems later. As searing as fresh grief is, the recovery is swifter when we face our loss.

Within two months, it was evident he wasn't propelled by strength at all. Not only was this former church deacon suddenly hanging out in the local bars, but he persuaded his new girlfriend to go to Florida with him. His family was horrified—and more than a little angry. How could he do this to their mother's memory? How could he decide not to live by the same rules he had always insisted his sons live by? What had happened to the dad they knew?

And that's the whole point—since he couldn't cope with the reality of his loss, he had to mask it over and become someone they didn't know. The one they knew wasn't as strong as they had thought. He knew that too and had to substitute another, lesser set of principles.

Another route this masking can take is by the person becoming self-centered. The pain he is trying to hide is so great he doesn't have room for anyone else's pain. But rather than say, "I can't handle that; I have enough problems of my own," he'll mask it with harshness. Barbara recalls her father's response to their neighbor's accident:

"Anybody who doesn't have the sense to stay off the roads on Memorial Day deserves just what he got."

Any of these inappropriate responses can result in greater problems later. As searing as fresh grief is, the recovery is swifter when we face our loss.

CHAPTER SIX

Talking to Children About Death

The most important thing we can do for a grieving child is talk to him—and listen to his observations. Children have many questions they often can't articulate. But a concerned adult can help them sort through conflicting emotions.

I learned one thing quickly—a child will have *more* problems if she can't cry. Jay had cried as soon as I told him his dad had died, but Holly was in a fog for days. She even fell asleep on the way to the cemetery and was blurry-eyed at the graveside service. The next morning she had hives so badly I kept her home from school. For much of that day, I held her on my lap even though she was eight years old. We both needed that quiet closeness.

From my personal and professional experiences I've learned some important steps in helping children:

Tell the Child Right Away

I told both children their dad had died within minutes of my walking in the door from the hospital. As difficult as that was, it gave an explanation for my tears, the presence of their grandparents and the endless phone calls. It also confirmed they were part of the family.

Be Truthful

Many times a parent, thinking death is too stark for the child, gives an unhealthy explanation such as "Mother's gone on a long trip." That's not only a lie, but it postpones having to tell the truth. Meanwhile, the child may feel resentful because her mother didn't say good-bye.

Along with truthfulness comes the necessity of thinking the way a child does. When Carl's wife was killed in a car accident, he told 3-year-old Dona her mommy was with Jesus. But when Dona's Sunday School teacher held up the traditional picture of Jesus with the children, Dona burst into tears. "Where's my mommy? My daddy said Mommy's with Jesus, but she's not there!"

While being truthful, we have to say "dead" and "died." But we don't like those words. We'd much rather use "passed away" or "lost" or "expired." But flowers "pass away," puppies are "lost" and parking meters "expire." People die.

I remember when my Uncle Curt died a couple of hours before I arrived at the hospital. I stood in the hallway outside his ICU cubicle, staring at the drawn blinds. I knew intellectually what the closed room meant, but I couldn't absorb the reality.

A nurse approached me and said, "Mr. Farley expired

this afternoon at 4:30." I stared at her stupidly for a moment, so she repeated her announcement. It still didn't register right away. How much better it would have been if she had just gently said, "I'm sorry, but Mr. Farley died this afternoon."

I was so aggravated she'd used an impersonal word about my uncle that when I arrived home, I looked up "expire." It comes from the Latin word meaning "to breathe out." When a person dies, the last breath they had taken comes out, so *medically* the nurse was correct in what she said. But it sounded so impersonal.

Another inappropriate euphemism is "lost." I don't say I've "lost my husband"; my husband *died*. I'm also not one of those pious widows who says, "Oh, I haven't 'lost' my husband; I know just where he is!"

My friend Renie Smith told me about a couple—we'll call them the Kidds—who used to shop at Klingman's Furniture Store in Grand Rapids. Whenever one of their many grandchildren was about to get married, they'd venture into the store, enjoy looking at all the displays and then select some large item as the wedding gift. One summer it seemed as though they were in the store every few weeks, but then four, maybe five, months passed.

Finally one afternoon, their favorite clerk saw Mrs. Kidd by the clock display.

"Mrs. Kidd! How nice to see you again. How are you?"

"Oh, not very well, dear. I've lost my husband."

"Oh, this place is so big that happens all the time. You just sit over here and I'll have him paged. We'll find him in a jiffy."

Stunned silence surrounded Mrs. Kidd for several moments. Finally she said, "No, dear. I mean my husband died."

I'm sure neither of them forgot *that* conversation.

Part of being truthful with the child is to let him see you hurt. One of the men in our Sunday School class was killed in a car accident. His wife, left with a baby and two preteens, was so busy during the day she refused to give in to her grief until the children were asleep. As a result, they never saw her cry. That didn't translate as "strength" to her fifth grader. He interpreted it as not caring, but didn't verbalize the thought until his late teens when he threw that at her during one of their arguments.

Share with the child the verses of Scripture that comfort you. Even preschoolers benefit from hearing that God cares for us so much He gave us verses to help us through painful situations. My favorite passages include God's promise in Romans 8:35-39 that nothing—not even death—can separate us from his love. Psalm 23:4 helps us remember that the valley is the *shadow* of death.

First Thessalonians 4:13-18 shows our hope of the resurrection. The thought that I'm going to see my beloved clown again offers enormous comfort. And even though marriages won't continue in heaven, surely I can give him an honest-to-goodness hug in greeting—without having to worry about his painful shingles!

Tell Only What the Child Can Handle

Greg was pinned in the wreckage of his car when he slammed into the back of an eighteen-wheeler on a Detroit area expressway. He died before the fire department could get the "Jaws of Life" machinery to the accident and before the morphine shot administered by the emergency crew could take effect. His parents wisely chose not to tell his younger brother the awful details.

I, too, initially spared Jay and Holly the details of their dad's death, telling them only that a blood clot hit his lungs and he died. Almost three years later, Jay asked if his dad had been in a lot of pain. I quoted a doctor who said that type of pulmonary embolsion is just as though the "lights went out." I don't know if that's true, but I take comfort in it. I saw Don's body arch, I heard the strangling sounds

---

Try to avoid saying things such as, "Grandpa just went to sleep." A five-year-old may start thinking, "If I go to sleep will I die too?"

(even these years later, my breathing is tense as I type this), and I know that even if the pain was intense, death came quickly. That's all I could tell Jay. And that was enough since it settled his mind on the issue.

Try to avoid saying things such as "Grandpa just went to sleep." Grandpa may very well have died peacefully in his sleep, but think how that sounds to a child. It isn't uncommon to have the child's sleeping patterns disturbed after a family loss as she equates sleep with death. A five-year-old may start thinking, "If I go to sleep will I die too?"

Encourage Children to Express Feelings

Often parents are so afraid of emotion, they insist their children suppress it too. In my first experience with losing someone I loved, I had the good fortune not to be hindered in that expression—but only because no one saw me. I was six years old when my great-grandmother,

"Grandmaw," died in Harlan County, Kentucky. The call came at noon. After my mother hung up the phone, tears fell on her apron bib as she stirred the potatoes and onions. When I asked what was wrong, she shook her head, unable to talk.

Finally I said, "Grandmaw died, didn't she?" I don't know where that came from. Perhaps I'd overheard one of the relatives say she was "bad off." Or perhaps it's my first evidence of that intuitive word of knowledge that hangs over me. But I went into my parents' bedroom, sobbing as I threw my six-year-old self across their white chenille bedspread. Gradually the choking knot in my throat eased.

But when I was 15, I was forced to grieve a different way. My dear elderly neighbor, Minnie Schumacher, died after a lengthy illness. I had stayed nights with her for two months after an intruder broke into her home. Supposedly, I was there to provide company and security for her, but she, in turn, gave me the personal attention I needed as the oldest child in a large family.

Our Saturday breakfasts in her sunny kitchen were the highlight of my week. We'd have oatmeal or eggs on her ancient flowered china and finish the meal with cinnamon-laden hermit cookies. Over cups of green tea she'd ask about my classes, then tell me about her school days at the turn of the century. When she died, I felt as though I'd lost my best friend.

Because of my special friendship with her, her niece Doris asked me to sit with the family. When I told my dad, he had quick advice for me: "Well, don't put on a show. You won't see those people crying and carrying on."

I certainly hadn't planned to "put on a show," but fighting back tears was too great of a tension. Within a few weeks, I developed deep red blotches on my face and neck. The doctor called it a "reaction" and prescribed medication. I wish society had had a better understanding of stress-related diseases back then. Children who are allowed to express emotion not only fare better at the time but will develop stronger patterns for coping with stress later.

Allow Children to Attend the Funeral

When I worked at the funeral home, we were constantly asked if children should attend the service. We always encouraged their being included. Not only do they need to feel part of the family unit, but they also have their questions about funerals answered. Of course, I'm thinking of the "normal" funeral—lots of silence broken only by the occasional stifled sob. If the family traditions include screaming, fainting, hugging the corpse or jumping into the grave, I wouldn't recommend that young children attend.

But while it's important they be included in the traditions, they need breaks from the intensity of the funeral home. At one point, I looked around for Holly and discovered she was standing on tiptoe by her dad's casket, trying to warm his cold hands with her own little ones. I asked my brother, Mitch, to take both children out for a hamburger and a rowdy romp in the park.

The adults can gain from the children's insight too. When my grandmother died in 1979, Don and I decided four-year-old Holly and six-year-old Jay would attend the funeral with us. During the drive to Kentucky, we reminded them of the biblical description of heaven, emphasizing that Mama Farley—the part we couldn't see—was already with the Lord.

Then we told them about the part they *would* see. She'd be lying in a big box, called a casket, surrounded by flowers. Many people would be in the room, we said, and some would be crying because Mama Farley couldn't talk to them anymore.

Trying to anticipate all they would see, we explained that some people would touch her hands or kiss her good-bye for, according to Southern belief, such action prevented bad dreams about the person. We stressed that no one would make them kiss her, but they could touch her hands if they wanted to.

We talked about the sad hymns the people would sing, what the minister would do, and the procession of cars to the cemetery. Then, most important of all, we asked if they had any questions. Jay was concerned with practical matters such as how the men put the casket into the ground. But Holly merely stared at us, her eyes big with silent wonder.

At the funeral home, we gripped the children's hands and walked into the flowered area. I studied Mama's dear, ancient face and thought of the godly example she'd been throughout my childhood. I remembered the skinned knees and wounded pride she had often healed with her hugs and fresh gingerbread. Still years away in my thoughts, I was startled by Holly's question.

"Is she breathing?" she whispered.

We hadn't anticipated that one. And her question required more than a quick no. Suddenly this business of trying to explain death to *myself* had become difficult. How could I make a child understand?

"Well, Holly . . . . " I stalled, searching for something both simple and theologically sound.

Jay then turned from his study of the casket handles to face his little sister. "No, Holly, she's not breathing.

Remember? The breathin' part's in heaven."

Since that day in April almost 11 years ago, I've had to stand before all too many caskets. But even with tears running down my cheeks, I'm comforted as I remember a little voice confidently announcing, "The breathin' part's in heaven." If I'd had a quick answer for Holly that day I would have missed Jay's.

Take the Child to the Cemetery

Most of us need an object where we can direct our grief. If the person has already been buried, it's important that the child be taken to the grave—if he wants to go. Not only will he have his questions answered, but he gets a sense of the universality of sorrow as he sees the rows of stones— each one representing heartaches.

Earl's mother died when he was 10. He moved through the typical haze during the preparations, but on the morning of the funeral refused to attend the service. The grandmother, concerned about how it would look to the community if he didn't attend, promptly insisted he "straighten up." A family friend wisely—and gently—stepped in, offering to stay with him. All that afternoon the two of them walked the tree-shrouded sidewalks of the village, the friend gently asking questions and encouraging the child to talk.

After several weeks of the friend's continued interest, Earl finally consented to visit the grave. Beneath those stately oak trees, a 10-year-old boy sobbed as the adult stood with an arm around his shoulders. Years later, as he recalled the scene, Earl expressed gratitude for the older man's understanding of a child's needs.

Not all of the grave visits will be this traumatic. Usually

it merely answers questions. In our early childhood, my brother, sisters and I knew Dad's father had been killed in a coal mine accident. But it had nothing to do with us until we stood by his headstone.

I imagined the mule-drawn wagon moving up the hill, and our dad, the somber two-year-old, watching the mysterious procedure of lowering the wooden box into the ground. Suddenly the unknown grandfather became a person to me and I understood my father's longings for a boyhood home. But the insight would never have come without the visit to a Kentucky hillside grave on a sunny afternoon.

Let the Child Talk

Even though Holly hadn't been able to cry after her dad died, she wanted to tell her classmates what had happened. Her teacher wisely allowed her to do just that. She stood in front of the class, her voice soft and her eyes downcast. Expressing her loss helped her deal with the reality of it.

How many times have we approached the adult at the funeral home and ignored the child standing nearby? It's important that he too be allowed to talk, explaining how his grandpa died or sharing some of his special memories. Not only does that attention acknowledge his place in the family but it acknowledges his grief as well.

When E. Ross Adair died, his then eight-year-old grandson Andy quietly tucked a picture of himself with a note in his grandpa's jacket pocket. When Marion, his grandmother, saw him, she praised his action and suggested the other grandchildren might like to do that as well. What started as one lonesome little boy's expression of love for his grandfather became a beautiful healing activity for all of the grandchildren.

Encourage Communication

I had learned from Jay's response to his dad's chemotherapy IV that lack of verbalization didn't mean lack of questions. Thus, after Don's death I tried to get both children to talk. Looking at the experience through eyes that are now older, I see some interesting things.

Jay was able to talk—and cry—about his loss immediately. During the next six months, he worked through several levels of a 10-year-old's grief, then apparently made a decision to go on with his life. Now six years later, he finds my attempts to get them to talk about their dad tedious.

Holly, on the other hand, still has some things she needs to deal with—not only did she lose her dad but she lost the dream of what her life would have been. Major events, such as her thirteenth birthday or eighth-grade graduation, trigger that loss for her again.

Be There

This is the young widow's greatest complaint: "Where are all the men who said they'd help father my son?" Long ago I learned that what people think they'll do—or even wish they could do—is far different than what they can do. Having already survived numerous broken promises in my life, I took a "wait and see" attitude toward all those made in the funeral home.

One relative called, asking me to tell Jay and Holly he was going to always be there for them. As evidence of that, he was going to write them every week—and asked me to tell them that too. I wisely chose not to. He wrote only two notes, even after both children had expressed their appreciation. People can not be all we want them to be—just as we can't be all they need us to be.

The need of fathering for their children is the very concern that drives many widows raising young sons alone to remarry—often with traumatic results. I remember the young woman whose husband died in an accident, leaving her with a 13-year-old son and eight-year-old daughter. As we talked, she said her greatest fear was how to raise her son to be a man: "How do I teach him to spit without getting it on his chin?" She remarried the next year, but the tension was so great between her son and new husband that she finally sent the child to live with his widowed grandmother.

Remarriage didn't solve that situation; it merely created greater ones. Children need time to work through the depth of their loss. In the case of this young lad, he was angry because he hadn't been able to say good-bye to his father. So how could he say hello to a stepfather?

Meeting that need for fathering is where the church can make a major difference in a child's life. I'm not suggesting that one man absorb all of the responsibility, but if several deacons or the father's friends would include the son even once a month with their own family, it would make a marvelous difference. I'm thankful for our friends who did invite Jay to sporting events or on camping weekends. And I'm realistic enough to know the extra effort it took to include an outsider. I especially appreciate it because I then found it so hard to ask for help.

I remember the Father/Son Banquet we had at our church. Since several sports figures, including Kent Benson of the Detroit Pistons, were going to be there, Jay casually mentioned he wanted to go. I couldn't ask one of our friends to include Jay because I knew they'd want to enjoy the special evening with their own sons. And I didn't blame them.

Since I wasn't into Rent-a-Boyfriend, I had no choice

but to take Jay myself. Being the only woman in attendance at an all-male event didn't bother me *until* we walked into the hall and I realized we didn't have assigned seats. I would have to approach a tableful of men and ask if we could join them. Argh!

With shaking knees, I put on my brightest smile, approached an available table, and asked, "Are you gentlemen secure enough to allow a woman to sit at your table?" (I cringe now to think of that statement, but it was produced by fear rather than arrogance.) They laughed and welcomed us, but in that moment I made up my mind to make sure I had a weekend trip planned when the next banquet arrived.

For many families any display of emotion is the same as "loss of control." But by helping the child deal with rampant emotions today, we have strengthened the future adult.

Affirm the Child's Feelings

The most common adult reaction to the child's expression of an emotion other than sadness is "Don't feel like that!" Normal emotions may include anger—even at the deceased parent, guilt and relief. The adult's negative response adds greater turmoil to the child's unvoiced emotions. Feelings aren't conjured up by the child, they just *are*.

Two weeks after Don's death, we three were driving to church for the midweek service. In the silence, Holly suddenly said, "I'm *so* angry!"

Anger was not what I wanted to hear right then. I was missing Don, convinced I couldn't raise our children without his laughter and not at all sure I was going to survive my own grief. In the midst of all that, I was supposed to continue teaching, pay bills and be the strong person everyone thought I was. But that night I was too tired to say anything other than, "Why are you angry, Holly?"

She didn't answer for a long moment, so I said, "Are you angry at God for taking your daddy?"

Long silence again. Finally she mumbled, "No."

"It's OK if you are angry at Him."

More silence, then she said, "No. 'Cause He helps us."

We stopped at the light at Lilly and Joy roads. "Are you angry at your daddy?" Silence. "He didn't want to leave, honey. He did everything he could to stay with us. He wanted to watch you and Jay grow up."

"I know." More silence, then, "I'm not angry at him."

"Well, do you know who you *are* angry at?" I held my breath. Surely she was angry at *me* since I was supposed to be taking care of her dad. Instead she gave one of her exasperated huffs.

"I'm angry at Adam and Eve. None of this would have happened if they hadn't disobeyed God!"

Her solution may seem rather simplistic, but it gave her someone at whom she could direct that anger. Being able to verbalize pain is the first step toward resolving it. That sounds rather easy, but for many families any display of emotion is the same as "loss of control." But by helping the child deal with rampant emotions today, we have strengthened the future adult.

CHAPTER SEVEN

Coping with Normal Depression

One of the most common results of grief is depression. It often originates in one of several ways.

Physical Illness

The one caring for the ill person battles the disease right along with him. This is one of those "Which came first: the chicken or the egg?" areas. Do we become ill because we're depressed? Or do we become depressed because we're ill?

We do know stress lowers our bodies' ability to fight disease. We can all think of cases where a seemingly strong widow died from breast cancer or a heart attack the year after her husband died. It's even more common for the survivor to have lowered resistance and to catch every germ going by. The illness that develops from stress is real—it's not something we dream up to gain sympathy.

My stress managed to burn out some central core,

allowing lupus—an internal cousin to arthritis—to sideline me for a year. It's still very much with me, but my internist—who first suggested chemotherapy (No thanks!)—and I have agreed that mine is controllable so far with rest and regular servings of brown rice. I'm thankful for how far I've come. I remember the nights of getting up to give Don his medication and having to grip the wall as I walked because of the pain in my legs and feet.

Not being able to continue with usual activities certainly causes depression and creates more stress. Doris Schumacher, my dear 85-year-old friend, has lost the two activities she most enjoys—reading and walking—because of her deteriorating eyesight. She was the one whose example more than 33 years ago encouraged me to become a teacher. Now she's teaching me how to grow older. Together we lament what she has lost, but then she quickly reminds me she has much to be thankful for. It sounds simplistic, but by concentrating upon what she can still enjoy— phone chats, visits with friends and afternoons in the sunny courtyard—she continues to fight the depression that could easily envelop her.

One final comment about depression: it is often not something to "snap out of," especially when it's caused by a chemical imbalance. If a family member is still depressed months after a family death, by all means make an appointment with the doctor. His advice and simple medication often help quickly.

Guilt

We discussed the three types of guilt—true, false and misplaced—at length in a previous chapter, but I want to emphasize here their impact upon depression.

I'm one of those who can handle a crisis but can't handle guilt. I learned a long time ago I might as well give in to a family gathering rather than suffer for days (weeks!) afterward. Example: It's late Friday afternoon and I'm typing the final corrections for the article that must be in the 5 P.M. mail. Then after a nice dinner with Jay and Holly, I'm looking forward to working on the grief seminar I'm presenting to the Baptist deacons tomorrow morning and going to bed early—for once. Then the phone rings.

"Are you busy, honey?" It's my mother.

"Never too busy to talk," I confess. "What's happening."

"Well, your uncle arrived this afternoon."

"That's wonderful. Give him my love. Maybe we can stop over Sunday afternoon to say hello."

"Well, honey," she begins, and my stomach knots. "He's going to be here just for tonight."

I glance at the page still in my typewriter. No, I'm going to be tough this time. "Oh, I'm sorry I'm going to miss him, but I'm giving a seminar tomorrow morning and I still have several points I want to work on."

If Almighty God, in His perfection, will forgive imperfect me, I'd be foolish to reject that gift.

Sigh. Pause. Do I hear her wiping tears from her eyes before she speaks? "I know, honey," she says. "I told him you're busy and probably wouldn't be able to come over. But I wish you could. He hasn't been feeling well lately."

She has won. "Set three extra plates, Mother. We'll be there in two hours."

We chuckle over such universal scenes, but guilt can

keep us trapped in depression, unless we take certain steps to free ourselves:

The first step in being free of that power is to recognize it.

The second is to accept it as a universal problem.

The third is to confess it and let it go.

When I've confessed my guilt but still have trouble letting it go, I quote 1 John 1:9 to myself: "If we confess our sins, he is faithful and just to forgive us our sins, and to cleanse us from all unrighteousness." If almighty God, in His perfection, will forgive imperfect me, I'd be foolish to reject that gift.

Anger Turned Inward

The typical definition of depression is "anger turned inward." Our giving in repeatedly to depression at the beginning may be by choice, but as the patterns are set, the brain releases toxins that set up a chemical imbalance, resulting in clinical depression that calls for medical intervention.

Don gave in to total depression for one day. The next morning he said, "Well, I tried being bummed yesterday and it was so horrible I'm not going to be depressed again. I guess I'll just have to show these doctors they're wrong." And that's when they were saying he had as little as two weeks to live!

So I ask these questions. How much of Don's extra time was due to his personal fight and how much was God's grace? If I give more credit to Don, am I taking away from God's miracle? Or, if I give all the credit to God, am I denying the power of the personal fight? If so, then I'm heaping guilt upon those who truly want to get well but can't.

I don't have the answers, but I know the One who does. And it's alright to ask as long as we're willing to listen to the answer.

Self-Effort

This is the feeling that we must do everything ourselves—a conviction that weighs heavily on the shoulders of many. Believe it or not, the Superwoman image is no longer popular. We don't have to do everything.

If each of us would use just the gifts she's been given, every job would be met—and no one would have to feel as though she's carrying the load alone. God doesn't ask for perfection. He merely asks for us.

On my fortieth birthday, friends teased me about being over the hill. But I welcomed the milestone. "Hey, I'm glad I'm 40," I said. "When I was in my 30s I was always trying to prove something to someone. Now I'm free to be exactly who I am."

Freedom emerges when we don't play games—and when we don't have to carry all those burdens ourselves. If we allow Him to, the Lord helps us through this thing loosely called "life." We don't have to carry our burdens alone—and we don't have to be everything to everybody.

We're at our best when we're allowed to use *our* talents. God has given us different talents, but we limit ourselves. If we can't balance our checkbooks, we think we're stupid. If we can't play the piano or speak in front of groups, we think God doesn't have a spot for us in the church. Wrong.

If each of us would use just the gifts she's been given, every job would be met—and no one would have to feel as though she's carrying the load alone. God doesn't ask for perfection. He merely asks for us.

Wrong Perspective

It's important that we talk to others to get their point of view.

In the weeks following Don's death, memories of his dying tormented me. As his back had arched, I—the doer and the supposedly strong one—had been relieved that the doctors rushed past me. Obviously, I'd watched too many Hollywood scenes of the wife cradling the husband, whispering words of comfort and strength. Real deathbed scenes aren't always so peaceful—and I was tormented by my uselessness.

During one of Morrie and Gert Driesenga's calls, they asked a sincere, "How are you doing?" I cried as I expressed my frustration. Morrie spoke first and gave me that different perspective I needed. "You didn't abandon him. You got out of the way so those who knew what to do could help."

It was a simple statement, but it carried profound comfort.

Adjustment Reactions

In the face of stress, we have to adjust or we'll get depressed. My motto for my schedule is "analyze and adjust." Neither my health nor my sanity will allow me to accomplish everything I want to do or even should do, so I adjust by setting priorities. What has to be finished today? What can wait until next week?

In one of life's wild coincidences, I had just typed the previous sentence when Jay called me downstairs. The outside panel of our thermopane sliding door had suddenly—and inexplicably—shattered. That's not exactly what I needed as I plowed through a dozen major projects, including leaving in three days to speak at the Maranatha Christian Writers' Conference in Muskegon, Michigan and meeting a deadline at *Christian Herald* magazine.

When I saw the glass, I gasped first. We're all allowed to do that! Then I examined the door and discovered the second panel was intact; it would hold until after I'd taken care of the other obligations.

How does this relate to grief? We have to adjust to all of the new responsibilities suddenly thrust upon us. When Don died, my grief was compounded by single parenting, and I wanted to run away to Tahiti or Kentucky. But one of my friend's comments gave me the proper perspective: "Just keep the kids clean and fed; the rest of it can wait."

Learned Behavior

Children learn how to handle stress by watching us. And we have learned how to handle stress by watching our parents. My mother would have reacted to that shattered pane of glass in the same way I just did—gasp, look at it, sigh and go on with her activities until she could do something about it.

I remember the noon one of my cousins burst into our kitchen. She had run from her house—several blocks away. All she could sob was something about "water" and "ceiling."

My mother drove her home to see what the problem was. The faucet on the basement pipes had jarred open, spraying water everywhere. Mother shut off the water and then brought the still whimpering bride back to our place for lunch.

Both had reacted as they had seen their own mothers react in similar situations. But I'm thankful we don't have to be bound by our early environment. And we don't have to be overcome by depression.

CHAPTER EIGHT

Surviving the Loss

For the first two months after Don died, I couldn't stand to
be downstairs in the family room—alone—after Jay and
Holly went to bed. So I'd go upstairs when they did, but I'd
take a stack of books with me. I read everything I could
find about grief, hoping to find something to help me get
over it. I hadn't learned yet that grief isn't something we
get *over* but *through*. As much as we want to be rescued
from the smothering feelings of panic, the only Person
who can walk on that lonesome path of sorrow with us is
the Lord. As we seek His answers, He will supply His
strength. Meanwhile, we *can* choose to turn toward healing.

Face the Loss

It's OK to hurt. You aren't damaging your testimony if you
cry. It's OK to miss someone we love. Remember, even
Jesus wept—at the tomb of Lazarus, over Jerusalem and
undoubtedly in the garden.

Scholars have pondered the reasons why Jesus wept at the tomb of His friend Lazarus. Was He weeping out of sorrow? Out of compassion for the sisters? Out of despair at their lack of faith? I think He was weeping because He knew Lazarus would have to go through death again. Jesus didn't promise us eternal *earthly* life—Lazarus wasn't being called back forever, just for a brief time.

So if Jesus—the Son of God—can cry, it's OK for me—a frail, imperfect human—to cry.

In facing the grief, it helps to remember that some of the dumbest things are going to get to you. For 16 and a half years, Don and I shared the towel rack. One hand towel hung in the middle with our separate wash cloths on either side—Don's on the left. A couple of days after the funeral, I was putting fresh towels up. Just as I started to put the two washcloths on either side of the hand towel, it hit me that I didn't need to hang *two* washcloths on the rack—Don wasn't coming back.

Talking through that loss with a trusted friend or a trusted grief therapist is an important first step in healing. Those who try to ignore this step—whether because it's too painful or because they think "good" Christians don't cry—often battle stress and depression later.

Recognize That Pain Comes with the Territory

Something healthy happens when we say, "This hurts!" Releasing that pain may be as dramatic as sobbing on the kitchen floor, as intense as crying all evening after the children are in bed or as quiet as a deep sigh when a young family reminds us of what we've lost.

Southerners have an expression to describe the intangible longing that occasionally sweeps over us; "feeling homesick and lonesome." Even as exciting as it is to be an evangelical editor in New York, I long for all I've lost. But I don't want my Canton, Michigan house back; I want those *years* back!

The only immediate cure I've found for that pain is the Bible. Every emotion humans are capable of is recorded there. Immediately Psalm 74:1 comes to mind: "Why hast thou cast us off for ever?" Once we've accepted the reality of our situation, we can begin to work through it with the Lord's help.

Accept the Universality of Suffering

Again Jesus is our chief example. Hebrews 4:15 *(NIV)* says, He was "tempted in every way, just as we are—yet was without sin."

This verse is usually interpreted to stress the temptations He faced and overcame, but I find comfort in the phrase "just as we are." He was totally divine, yet totally human too. He cried and grew weary and hungry—but always responded with holiness.

I'm not the first widow nor will I be the last. Once the Donald J. Aldrich family was the Perfect Family. By the world's standard's, we had it all—and I thought we would have those glory days forever. Now I know all too well that everyone is going to suffer at one time or another.

The Easter after Don died, Pete and Gail Collins—dear friends in Chattanooga—invited us to spend the holiday with them. One afternoon, Gail and I took our four children to Lookout Mountain, where a major battle of the Civil War had occurred. In the museum, I read a Confederate soldier's letter that said in part, "Some of us are rich and some are poor. Some are old and some are young. But we all bleed the same."

The universality of suffering was illustrated in another

way the following Christmas. All of us have our pet peeves. One of mine happens to be grave blankets. What are they keeping warm anyway? But Don had always liked them, saying they were a symbol that the person under them had been loved. So, of course, I bought one and anchored it on top of his frozen soil the week after the funeral. With tears running down my cheeks, I whispered, "You were truly loved, Donnie."

The next year, I made my purchase as soon as they were displayed at the local florist shop. But even as I paid for it, I complained about the pagan practice of grave blankets. The Greek owner listened politely to my complaints and then asked, "What if you had to wash the bones of your husband?"

"What?!"

He nodded. "On my island in Greece only the wealthy own the graves of their family. The rest of us must rent the ground for three years. At the end of that time, we dig up our dead, wash the bones, put them in a small box and place them into the burying wall. I did that for both of my parents. Grave blankets aren't such a bad custom."

Emphatically I agreed.

Recognize the Power of Guilt

One favorite story of every grief therapist is of two men whose mothers died in the same hospital. As the chaplain talked to them, the first son blamed himself for not having sent his mother to Florida, saying the cold weather had killed her. A few minutes later the chaplain talked to the second man, who blamed himself for *his* mother's death, saying he shouldn't have sent her to Florida because the change in temperature and water had been just too much for her system!

For those still hounding themselves with the "should haves," they're dealing with false guilt—the kind the Enemy loves to use—and must release it. One way is by saying aloud, "This is false guilt and is not from God." Then as they ask God to comfort—and keep talking to Him—the peace will come.

It's OK to Treat Yourself Kindly

One of the most common expressions of false guilt is the feeling the griever has that she shouldn't be good to herself. After all, her husband is dead; how can she buy a new dress or go out to dinner? But that's just it—we aren't dead; our husbands are. And taking care of ourselves is one of the best ways to work through the swarming guilts. That means it's OK to take a morning walk and OK to buy a new dress.

This is a difficult area for me because my whole childhood training has been in how to take care of others—a husband, babies, relatives. A few years ago, the ethnic mother jokes were popular: "Don't worry about me, dear. You go to Florida. I'll be fine. I'm happy to sit here in the dark—all by myself." Believe me, most of us can match those antics any time. So how do we break away from it? By giving ourselves little verbal pep talks: "I took good care of Don, now it's time to take good care of myself."

Some grievers resume abandoned hobbies. Others of us finally set aside an hour away from our family. During the spring and summer, I have no trouble getting up at 5:00 A.M. to walk for two miles. But the winter months pose another problem. Since walking is enjoyable only when I can see the interesting things around me, I had to find other ways—such as walking at noon—to get that enjoyable trek in.

Guard Your Health

This is a warning I didn't heed. I went from long months of fighting cancer by Don's side to facing daily challenges— and the future—alone. Not only was I worn out, but youth was no longer on my side. And in the midst of my grief I was still trying to help some of my relatives. I wish I'd said a few more times, "I'm sorry but I can't deal with that situation" or "I can't solve that problem for you; I'm still hurting."

I offer that advice hesitantly because I don't want widows suddenly to turn into self-centered whiners. But sometimes the best way we can feel good about ourselves is by not giving in to another's unreasonable request. It's OK to go to bed earlier than ever before—especially during the first few months. Grieving takes enormous energy, so your body needs more rest. We aren't *super* beings; we are *human* beings.

Both 1 Corinthians 3:16 and 6:19 proclaim that our bodies are temples of God's Holy Spirit. We've all heard the sermons that we, therefore, aren't to destroy that temple by smoking, drinking, adultery or overeating. But we can also destroy the temple by not resting, exercising or eating properly.

It's also important to keep in close communication with the Lord, so regrets and sins don't build up. Proverbs 28:13 *(NIV)* says: "He who conceals his sins does not prosper, but whoever confesses and renounces them finds mercy." Confession really *is* good for the soul.

Quite often when I speak, women tell me amazing things afterwards. I used to think they were convinced I had answers just because I had the nerve to speak in front of a group. But now I think they need someplace to dump the horrible hurts they carry. I've prayed with women struggling with guilt for their own sins as well as for those who were sinned against through incest, alcoholic parents, lonely childhoods, taunting relatives, constant moves, poverty, whatever. The stories never become stale because each one carries fresh suffering.

What if we stopped asking "Why me?" and concentrated upon "Why not me?" Why do we think we're supposed to get through this life without sorrow?

After we pray, I suggest they tell someone who can help them work through the various issues. Of course only the Lord can heal, but sometimes people are so hurt they need help hearing His voice.

Find the Silver Lining

Believe it or not, we do have the choice of whether we want to be better or bitter because of what we've experienced. What if we stopped asking "Why me?" and concentrated upon "Why *not* me?" Why do we think we're supposed to get through this life without sorrow? Think of Job's observation: "Shall we accept good from God, and not trouble?" (Job 2:10, *NIV*)

Let's allow that grief to make us better people as we learn from it and help others through their own pain. We can also help ourselves as we grab the importance of *this* moment and *this* day.

Whenever I think about the importance of attitude, I'm reminded of an old rabbinical story of nine men who were living in one room and not getting along very well. They called for the rabbi to settle their problems. He looked at their sorrowful faces and said, "I can solve your problem, but you must promise to do whatever I say. Agreed?"

The men glanced at each other and reluctantly nodded. The rabbi continued. "What you must do is get a goat to live here with you for one month. The problem will be solved after those 30 days."

Adding another creature to already crowded conditions wasn't the solution the men wanted, but they had promised. Several weeks later, the rabbi saw one of the men on the street. "Well, how are things with all of you now?"

The man beamed. "Oh, we're getting along great—now that we've gotten rid of the goat."

Setting goals is a tough area for most of us who grieve . . . . But life is not over. What do you want to be doing two years from now? . . . Whatever goals we have for the future have their roots in this moment.

Keep a Journal

Carl and Marilyn Amann—both of whose first spouses had died in accidents—took down our Christmas tree the day Don died, helping me clear the house for the arrival of relatives. As they hugged me good-night—promising to be back the next day—Carl insisted I verbalize my pain on paper. The first entry was scribbled: "How could my world have changed so suddenly in just these few hours.

Don died this afternoon. Died? He can't be dead—he's my best friend—my whole world."

Later I would have only enough strength to copy Jeremiah 10:19—"Woe is me for my hurt! my wound is grievous: but I said, Truly this is a grief, and I must bear it."

I remember one widow who wrote letters to her husband every day—just as she had when he was away on business trips. She wasn't denying his death and she knew the letters were going into her notebook rather than into the mailbox. But every night she wrote about what she and the children had done that day, told the neighborhood gossip or expressed frustration at the latest home and car maintenance problems. The routine provided a safety zone until she could face the future without him.

It's OK to Set Goals

Setting goals is a tough area for most of us who grieve. An important part of our very being was buried along with the person we loved. But life is *not* over. What do you want to be doing two years from now? Still sitting in the orange chair watching TV? Volunteering at the hospital? Working with teen drug addicts? Whatever goals we have for the future have their roots in this moment.

After Margo got over the initial pain of her son's traffic death caused by a drunk driver, she answered her own questions about the future by completing her degree and teaching high school. For the next 18 years, she had a direct influence upon several hundred teens a year.

Accept the Changes

For the first several weeks I refused to serve dinner at the family table. I simply couldn't face that fourth—empty—

chair. Instead, we three dined out or ate in the family room while we watched "M.A.S.H."

Then I decided I'd dodged the issue long enough. That evening, we sat at the table and put our hands toward each other for the blessing on the food. But the round table was too large and our hands didn't reach. We needed Don there. I covered my face with my hands and sobbed.

The next evening I faced the dinner hour with the same dread. But the three of us needed structure if we were going to retain our status as a family, so we sat at the table again. That time I sat in Don's chair—so I wouldn't have to look at its emptiness—and we didn't hold hands as we prayed. Gradually we became comfortable again in that setting.

The holidays took major changes. Don's favorite holiday meal was the traditional Thanksgiving dinner. But after he died, I couldn't cook if he wasn't there to say, "Great meal, San."

However, for Jay and Holly's sakes I couldn't spend the day in bed either. Several of our friends had invited us for dinner, but I didn't want to spend the day with someone else's Perfect Family. If I was going to compare myself to others, I wanted the comparison going in the right direction.

So I called the Salvation Army and offered to work. That was exactly the right decision; two minutes of watching single mothers, street people, the elderly and even families come in for dinner showed me another world.

The closest I came to tears that day was when the captain led us in a chorus before the dinner. The contrast of my previous Thanksgivings when I had cooked for Don and the relatives was just too much; I wanted to sob.

But I blinked back the tears as I looked at the others in the hall. What had they lost? What about the smiling lady with the white summerweight dress? Had she once cooked for a large family? Perhaps her husband had given her shoulders a tight squeeze and whispered "Great meal, hon."

Or how about that polite man in the shabby suit? Did he live in one of the downtown hotels and had he come for the company as well as the food? Gradually I set aside my own problems. I had discovered the difference between being miserable and acting miserably.

Another major change I made was giving myself permission to travel—especially in the summer. Don didn't want to leave Maranatha, and for us to have separate vacations was unthinkable. The first summer after his death, Jay and Holly and I drove to Kentucky to visit relatives I hadn't seen in years.

Of course not all the changes we make have to be that dramatic. Even something as simple as changing the bathroom colors from brown to peach can be satisfying. Or wearing purple instead of the pink he always purchased for you. The best changes are the ones we make in ourselves. Ephesians 4:31-32 *(NIV)* says, "Get rid of all bitterness, rage and anger, brawling and slander, along with every form of malice. Be kind and compassionate to one another, forgiving each other, just as in Christ God forgave you."

Learn to Forgive

I had trouble forgiving myself for "letting" Don die. Even though my extended care of him damaged my health, I was tormented by the thought I could have done more. One evening, I prayed, "What *didn't* I do?"

Within my spirit I heard the gentle reply: "You did all you could." As future self-accusations came, I recalled that thought and learned to let go of the rest.

Forgiving others was even more tricky though—especially as I thought of one of Don's relatives who ignored countless opportunities to encourage him. But I knew John 13:34-35 *(NIV)* wasn't to be trifled with: "A new commandment I give you: Love one another. As I have loved you, so you must love one another. All men will know that you are my disciples if you love one another."

Mark 11:25 *(NIV)* was just as relentless. "And when you stand praying, if you hold anything against anyone, forgive him, so that your Father in heaven may forgive you your sins."

Again prayer was my only refuge as I worked through complicated emotions. I'd love to report that my prayers were sweet and holy, but I was hurting too much. Like a scared, angry little kid, I listed years of accumulated gripes. And I had no safer place to dump all my misery than in the Lord's lap. I'm thankful that when He said, "Come unto me" (Matt. 11:28) He *didn't* add, "But make sure your attitude is right first."

Determined to be a good spiritual example for Jay and Holly, I set my jaw and continued sending notes, extending the usual invitations for dinner. Gradually I noticed that it become absolutely delicious to return "good for evil." Then the most amazing thing happened—my relationship with that relative became genuine. As I had supplied the right action—and continued to pray—the sincere attitude followed until I was able to forgive him even without his having asked. No dramatics. Just peace.

Help Others

Matthew 7:12 *(NIV)* states, "In everything, do to others what you would have them do to you, for this sums up the Law and the Prophets."

Since our Thanksgiving experience that first year after Don's death had been so positive, I called the Salvation Army again and offered to help at Christmas. But our scheduled day was so cold I couldn't get warm, even with my new coat tightly buttoned against the wind.

The first delivery was up a set of rickety steps to an apartment over a downtown store. An elderly woman opened the door cautiously, waiting for me to identify myself. Her eyes settled immediately upon the red Salvation Army badge pinned to my coat collar. Then she grinned as she saw Jay and Holly smiling at her.

She started to speak but instead cleared her throat several times as though she wasn't used to talking. Finally she gestured to the table in the middle of the one room serving as living room, bedroom and kitchen. I unpacked the small turkey, potatoes, canned green beans, cranberry sauce and rolls.

"Is all this for me?" she said. "Are you sure they haven't made a mistake? Why, that's a feast!" Her eyes suddenly sparkled.

I wondered how long it had been since that stark room had heard so many words.

"Oh, I know there's no mistake, " I said. "The social services director gave me your name himself."

Her aged face crinkled into a grin.

"Well, you tell that sweet young man I'd marry him in a minute if he were available."

We said our good-byes, and I went out the door happier than when I had climbed those dark stairs. But the next stops were to tired houses and more one-room apartments. We three carried in the bags, stayed momentarily to hear about grandchildren who looked like Jay and Holly, and heard excuses why adult children couldn't visit over the holidays. A "Merry Christmas" was said along with each good-bye, but I still wasn't any closer to peace.

I was cold, the weather was miserable, and I couldn't see that I was making a great difference in anyone's life. If we hadn't been delivering the groceries, someone else would have.

The last address was several miles south. Watching the snow swirl across the road, I started the car. The sooner we made this last delivery, the sooner we could get home. Some intangible wind cut through even the closely woven fibers of my new coat.

Jay and Holly were almost asleep by the time we reached the area. I steered with my left hand and groped for the address card. Glancing at the back, I noticed handwritten words under the category "Special needs." That space had been blank on the other cards, but this one plainly stated, "Large-size woman's coat."

I wished I'd seen that before we left. I could have chosen a coat off the rack against the back wall. With the rush of the holidays, no one else from the Salvation Army would make a special trip way out here just to deliver a coat. And I certainly wasn't going to offer my own on such a cold afternoon, even though I wore the same size.

At last we arrived at the address on the card. Years ago, the place must have been a cute cottage. Now it was only a tired, leaning shack. Its graying boards still showed signs of white paint, undoubtedly applied many years ago. An old car sat in the yard—up on blocks and tireless. I wondered if they had sold the tires to provide something else they needed.

As I shut off the ignition, Jay and Holly sat up and looked around. "Gosh, Mom," was Jay's only comment as he saw the house.

As we walked toward the front door, an elderly woman solemnly gestured toward the back. The front one was sealed with plastic to keep out December's subzero temperatures.

The three of us stamped our feet at the back steps as a man in his 70s held the door for us. "Don't worry about the snow," he said, but still we stamped—perhaps stalling for time.

Once inside, I set the bag on the kitchen table, trying not to notice the worn-out room. Everything was clean, but only near the walls were pieces of tile left. Those once in the middle of the room had been worn to the floorboards beneath. The curtains had been mended so many times the stitches made a pattern in the flimsy material.

The elderly couple thanked me repeatedly. All I had to do was smile and walk out the door. Instead, I found myself apologizing for not having brought a coat. The woman smoothed the sleeves of her old navy blue sweater and gave us an it's-OK smile.

It struck me she'd been disappointed so many times that another disappointment hardly mattered. Through the curtains I could see the snow blowing across the frozen driveway. Suddenly I took off my coat and said, "Here, try this one for the size."

She hesitated, then did as I asked. She even buttoned it and smiled at her husband as she turned to show him the back. It fit! I leaned forward to unpin the badge from the collar.

"Looks like you got yourself a coat," I stammered, afraid she wouldn't accept.

Instead, she hugged me and whispered, "God bless you, honey," as tears rolled down her cheeks.

Suddenly I was crying, too. What had been awkwardly offered was graciously accepted.

"Thank you for letting me do this," I whispered.

Her husband and Jay and Holly silently watched, not sure what to do. Soon we were out the door, waving good-bye to the old couple standing together.

As soon as the door closed, Holly turned to me. "Mom! It's freezing! And you gave away your coat!"

I felt like giggling.

"I know. Isn't it wonderful? Nobody needs two gray coats, anyway. And you know what? This is the warmest I've been all day!"

I gave Holly's shoulders a squeeze. Hysteria wouldn't threaten me again for a long time.

Take the Good from the Past into the Future

Second Corinthians 1:3-4 *(NIV)* reads, "Praise be to the God and Father of our Lord Jesus Christ, the Father of compassion and the God of all comfort, who comforts us in all our troubles, so that we can comfort those in any trouble with the comfort we ourselves have received from God."

In Genesis 50:20, Joseph talking to his brothers in Egypt, years after they had sold him to a caravan, says, "You intended to harm me, but God intended it for good to accomplish what is now being done, the saving of many lives" *(NIV)*.

God can—and will—bring His good out of any situation we give to Him.

Don had always taken care of the car's maintenance, so I knew only how to start the engine and where to pump the gas. He'd mentioned needing new tires soon but when he'd died, I couldn't think about them. A blow-out on the expressway forced me to deal with the issue. The next morning I was in the tire shop, nodding at appropriate times as the salesman explained treads and radials, *L*s and *K*s. The strain surely showed on my face.

"Why don't you grab a cup of coffee next door while the new tires are put on?" the young man suggested.

Once I was out in the sunshine, the tears ran down my face. "OK, God," I muttered, "I know Mama Farley would have said, 'There are some things that all we can do with 'em is bear 'em.' But I'm tired of being brave. I hate it that Don's dead! He should be helping me raise Jay and Holly. He should be making the financial decisions. I want some encouragement right now!"

I wiped my eyes and turned toward the restaurant. A young woman was standing by the open hood of her car. She insisted it would start again in another 10 minutes—after it cooled off. So we pushed it out of the way, and I invited her to have a cup of coffee with me.

Over the steaming cups, we made small talk. She asked if I was married. When I told her Don had died in December, I expected her to mutter, "Oh, I'm sorry."

Instead she shrugged. "How long were you married?"

"Sixteen and a half years."

She took a sip of her coffee. "Did you love him?"

"Yes, very much."

"Did he love you?"

I smiled. "Oh, yes."

Again she shrugged. "Then you've already experienced more love than most of us. Think of what you had instead of what you've lost."

Then she told about her divorce—the beatings, the custody battles, the continuing threats. Suddenly, she looked at her watch. "Hey, I gotta get to work. But thanks for listening. That helped a lot."

She was out the door before I could tell her how much *she* had helped me. God had certainly answered my prayer for encouragement—but not at all the way I had expected.

Get to Know Yourself Better

Don't be afraid of the quietness of your home. Don't go running from place to place—give yourself time to discover who you really are. And let each day shine! I love going for walks, especially on crisp days. But I always look for something unusual—orange and red bittersweet clinging to a tree limb or a red-leafed tree against a blue sky.

On my trip to the Middle East, I was frustrated by not being able to share the adventure with Don. Then one night I dreamed he was standing by my bed, laughing his unabashed belly laugh. "Ah, San," he said, "you're going to discover I never really died."

And that's true. His death taught me the value of laughter and the preciousness of *this* day. Now I cling to the Lord and try not to give in to the pain. This world is not the end. I will see my beloved clown again.